Acknowledgments

First of all, I'd like to thank my patient and greedy neighbors who lined up at the door for lunch nearly every day while I was testing recipes. The price of admission was simply an honest opinion, which they rendered eloquently, always being careful to "suggest" rather than complain or criticize. Helen Mildner; Dottie McGann; and Ernest, Robert, and Paul Tassoni all rendered indispensable tasting services. My mother, while visiting, also jumped in enthusiastically.

I'd also like to thank a number of people who helped with suggestions, ideas, discussions, and food or wines to taste: Pascal Vignau, executive chef at the Four Seasons Aviara Resort; his colleague Alessandro Serni, executive chef at the Four Seasons Aviara signature restaurant, Vivace; restaurateurs Neela Paniz and David Chaparro of the Bombay Café in Los Angeles; Greek wine importer Sotiris Bafitis; Greek cooking expert Diane Kolchilas; Sofia Perpera of Wines of Greece; Reno Christou, general in Manhattan; British-born Andrew Spurgin, executive director of Waters Catering in San Diego; Julian Contreras of Wine Street in Carlsbad, California; Beth Hensperger; and Gary Sehnert of Wines of Mexico.

In addition, I'd like to thank Holly Taines White, Lorena Jones, and Phil Wood of Ten Speed Press. Holly patiently edited the book and offered many useful and insightful suggestions; Lorena "took the bait" in the first place; and Phil enthusiastically supported the project.

I

Introduction

A couple of years ago, while researching a biography, I had occasion to spend three months away from home. I was in a rural setting, the weather was cold, and I brought one piece of cooking equipment that I thought might be particularly useful: a slow cooker.

I would get up in the morning, spend a bit of time cleaning and chopping, then consign the ingredients to the slow cooker for the day, while I wrote, interviewed, and kept appointments. At the end of the day, I'd lift the lid of the slow cooker, give the contents a stir, and breathe in the comforting smells emanating from the pot.

My experiments were quite simple: ingredients included beans, herbs from the small garden outside my door, a few root vegetables from the local market, and some good salt to enhance natural flavors. But when I returned home, my dishes became more lavish and more complicated. I began taking some of my favorite ethnic recipes and adapting them to the slow cooker, trying to stick as close as possible to the original renditions. And it wasn't hard to come up with recipes that would suit the slow cooker, as one-pot meals have been a part of cultures around the world for thousands of years.

Pottery, perhaps the greatest invention in terms of culinary evolution, was first developed around 6000 B.C.E. Humans learned how to mold earth and, by firing it at high temperatures, turn it into something that would endure. All that was needed was a suitable clay soil, some clever hands, and fire. From such simple ingredients emerged a world of vessels for storing and preparing foods and beverages.

With the development of earthenware cooking vessels, it was possible to combine and cook many

THE GOURMET
SLOW COOKER

THE GOURMET
SLOW COOKER

Simple *and* Sophisticated Meals
from Around *the* World

Lynn Alley

Photography by Paul Moore

TEN SPEED PRESS
Berkeley | *Toronto*

Ten Speed Press
PO Box 7123
Berkeley, California 94707
www.tenspeed.com

Distributed in Australia by Simon and Schuster Australia,
in Canada by Ten Speed Press Canada, in New Zealand by
Southern Publishers Group, in South Africa by Real Books,
and in the United Kingdom and Europe by Airlift Book
Company.

Cover and text design by Catherine Jacobes
Food styling by George Dolese
Food styling assistance by Elisabet de Nederlanden
Prop styling by Paul Moore and George Dolese

Library of Congress Cataloging-in-Publication Data
Alley, Lynn.
    The gourmet slow cooker : simple and sophisticated
meals from around the world / Lynn Alley.
       p. cm.
Includes index.
    ISBN 1-58008-489-3 (pbk.)
1. Casserole cookery. 2. Cookery, International. I. Title.
TX693 .A446 2003
641.8'21—dc21   2003006074

First printing, 2003
Printed in Hong Kong

2 3 4 5 6 7 8 9 10 — 07 06 05 04

To M., with all my love, always.

Contents

different ingredients in one container. The one-pot meal became a reality.

One of the first known one-pot meals has been analyzed by Dr. Patrick McGovern, an archaeologist and senior research scientist at the University of Pennsylvania Museum's Applied Science Center for Archaeology. His specialty is examining food and beverage residues from archaeological sites around the world. He has developed cutting-edge techniques for doing so, and has made many fascinating discoveries, among them the earliest known evidence of intentional wine making in northern Iran.

One of Dr. McGovern's most famous discoveries has been dubbed "The Midas Feast." In the 1950s, scientists first uncovered the remains of what appears to have been the funerary feast of an ancient Phrygian king near the city of Gordion in central Turkey. At the time of the initial discovery, scientists lacked the technology to analyze residues of the food and beverages found at the site, but were able to deduce that the tomb may have belonged to the King Midas of legend.

In 1998, nearly fifty years after that initial discovery, Dr. McGovern subjected the food and beverage residues found in Midas's funeral cauldron to analysis in his museum lab. His results were stunning, and showed us the contents of one of the world's earliest known one-pot meals on record.

The lab analysis showed that Midas's funereal meal, prepared around 800 B.C.E., consisted of stew simmered in an enormous bronze cauldron. Residues of a specific type of fatty acid and triglycerides indicated that the main ingredient was lamb or goat, while phenanthrene and cresol indicated that the meat had been grilled before it was cut off the bone and placed in the cauldron. Oleic and elaidic acids signified the presence of olives and/or olive oil. Traces of tartaric acid suggested the stew contained wine, while gluconic acid hinted at traces of honey. Residues of a high-protein pulse such as lentils were also present. There were also hints of anise and local herbs. (Read more about the Midas Feast at www.museum.upenn.edu/Midas/intro.html.)

Although Midas's stew was not likely to have been the first one-pot meal, it is irrefutable proof that the one-pot meal has been around for a very long time.

Over hundreds of years, the peoples of each region of the world found their own particular type of clay and adapted their local foods to the one-pot meal. This legacy is still to be found in almost every culture. In Mexico, *frijoles de la olla* ("beans from the pot") are cooked as they have been for hundreds of years: in a simple clay pot over an open fire. Many other countries, such as Greece, Italy, and France, maintain the tradition of clay-pot cookery. In some parts of the world, the pot has traditionally been a metal cauldron, but like the earthenware casserole, it remains a symbol of perpetual nourishment.

In our own kitchens, we have the opportunity to continue a long-standing tradition of creative one-pot meals, cooked in our own ceramic casserole. It may no longer be fueled by fire, but hopefully the ingredients are still prepared with care, concern, and the intent to nourish the body and give pleasure to the senses.

My goal with these recipes was to present fresh ideas a cut above the kind of food usually associated with slow cookers. I wanted to try a more gourmet approach, for people who appreciate simple meals, but don't want to sacrifice flavor and complexity. These recipes are some of my favorite one-pot meals from around the world updated for the slow cooker, and I've included beverage suggestions to make your dining experience more complete.

The Midas Feast

Serves 4 to 6

Here's my version of the Midas Feast, one of the earliest recorded one-pot meals.

Rinse the lentils thoroughly and place them in the slow cooker.

Combine the aniseed and cumin in a mortar or coffee grinder and grind to a coarse powder.

Heat a large sauté pan over medium-high heat and add the oil. In batches if necessary, add the lamb and cook, turning occasionally, for 7 to 10 minutes, until thoroughly browned. Using tongs, transfer the lamb to the slow cooker, arranging it on top of the lentils.

Add the onion to the pan and sauté, stirring frequently, for 10 to 15 minutes, until browned. Add the spice mixture to the onion and stir for 2 to 3 minutes. Add the wine to the sauté pan and stir to scrape up the browned bits from the bottom of the pan. Simmer for about 10 minutes, until the wine is reduced by one-third. Add the stock and honey and stir well. Pour over the lamb and lentils in the slow cooker.

Cover and cook on low for 4 to 6 hours, until the meat is very tender. Add the salt and serve the stew over the barley.

TO DRINK Master brewer Sam Calagione, owner of Dogfish Head Craft Brewery in Delaware, created Midas Touch Golden Elixir, a hand-crafted ancient ale, according to Dr. Patrick McGovern's specifications, using barley, honey, white Muscat grapes, and saffron. Read about it on www.dogfish.com. Or, serve a full-bodied red wine such as a California Zinfandel.

1 cup brown lentils

2 teaspoons aniseed or fennel seed

2 teaspoons cumin seed

3 tablespoons olive oil

2^1/$_2$ pounds lamb stew meat, cut into 1^1/$_2$-inch cubes

1 yellow onion, chopped

2 cups dry red wine or Midas Touch ale

1 cup chicken stock (page 101) or water

2 tablespoons honey

2 teaspoons salt

4 cups cooked barley (optional)

Tips for the Slow Cooker

Size and shape of the slow cooker. Today, most slow cookers are oval in shape, with the exception those under two quarts, which are generally round. All of the recipes in this book were tested in an oval five-quart slow cooker, unless otherwise specified. A few were tested in a round one and a half–quart cooker, and such recipes clearly indicate this fact.

Slow cooker safety. When slow cooking large pieces of meat, remember that they will take some time to come to temperature. This may pose a health risk as bacteria can continue to grow during the initial stages of cooking. Browning the meat in a sauté pan before slow cooking can jump-start the heating process and kill any bacteria on the surface of the meat. If you are particularly concerned about health risks, follow the USDA's recommendation of cooking such recipes on high for the first hour, and then decreasing the heat for the balance of cooking.

Speeding up your slow cooking. Most of the recipes in this book call for an initial sautéing of ingredients to impart some caramelization and flavor. In many cases, the outcome of the dish would not be adversely affected if you skipped this step and simply combined all the ingredients in the slow cooker at once.

Filling the slow cooker. Don't fill the insert of the cooker more than two-thirds to three-quarters full, or the food near the top will take too long to cook.

Placement of food in the slow cooker. Place those ingredients that take longer to cook, such as larger pieces of meat, carrots, or potatoes, near the bottom of the slow cooker.

Cooking temperature. Save the high setting for when you really need your dish cooked faster or for dishes that require a higher temperature, such as cakes. If you overuse the high setting, you'll find that all your food tastes the same: boiled. In general, simmer food on the low setting.

Variable cooking times. Be flexible; cooking times are not set in stone. Many factors may affect or alter a food's cooking time: the voltage of your cooker, the altitude, the time of year, the density of the ingredients, and the size of the cooker, just to name a few.

A chicken dish cooked for three or four hours will produce meat with relatively firm texture and recognizable parts, whereas the same chicken dish cooked for six to eight hours will yield meat that is falling off the bone. It's a matter of time and personal preference.

Preparing the slow cooker for a cake. To prepare the cooker to bake a cake, biscotti, or brownies, butter or oil the inside of the insert. Then cut a piece of waxed paper to fit into the bottom of the insert, and grease it as well.

Lifting the lid. Most slow cooker cookbooks caution against lifting the lid while a dish is cooking because the food will then take longer to cook. But I think that lifting the lid, smelling the food, and poking it around is half the fun of cooking. I highly recommend it. Stirring the pot falls into the same category.

Leaving the lid slightly ajar. When you want some of the liquid in the slow cooker to evaporate, or if you are baking a cake or biscotti and want the ingredients to dry out a bit, leave the lid slightly ajar. Doing so for the last few minutes of cooking also aids in developing a browned surface when baking cakes or cookies.

Turning the slow cooker. The entire surface of the slow cooker does not always heat evenly. All of my slow cookers seem to have hot spots. In most cases, variations in temperature make little difference, but when baking cakes or cookies, it can mean that one edge may darken more than the others. If this begins to happen, using pot holders, simply turn the insert in the cooker to allow for a more even cooking.

Eat the next day. Just about everything in this book tastes better the day after you make it, and this is true with most slow cooker recipes. For this reason, you may wish to make a soup or stew the day before you plan to serve it, then refrigerate it overnight.

Freezing your dishes. Many of the recipes in this book freeze well, with the exception of potatoes and creamed dishes.

Slow cooker cleanup. The surface of most ceramic slow cooker inserts is easy to clean. No need to use harsh abrasives. Soap and warm water, with a little elbow grease, should do it.

United States

American cooking is, fittingly, melting-pot cooking, with layer upon layer of distinct ethnic contributions. The original layers were based on our indigenous ingredients, such the beans and corn of the Southwest's earliest inhabitants, still to be found today in so many Tex-Mex and Southwestern dishes. The next layers came from the Spanish settlers in the Southwest, followed by the earliest English settlers in the northeastern part of the country.

As successive waves of immigrants washed into the United States, they often settled in geographic locations that looked like home, and brought their favorite dishes wit0h them. In addition, they brought seeds or young plants and animals for a renewable source of sustenance. Chicken probably arrived in the States with some of the earliest British settlers, while various people from Mediterranean countries brought grapevines here to plant. And because the immigrants chose regions that were similar to those at home, their plants and animals flourished.

Dishes that may have been recognizable at home, however, were soon transformed by equipment and ingredients available in the New World. Traditional one-pot meals, soups, and stews are found around the country today, many of them having recognizable origins in foreign countries, and many being uniquely American, such as succotash and Boston baked beans.

Gathered in this chapter are some of my favorite American one-pot meals, many of them traditional, and all of them typical American comfort food.

American Food and Drink

Just as traditions in American cookery come from many different cultures, so too do its beverage traditions. From the northern European influence

BOSTON BAKED BEANS | RED BEANS *and* RICE

POTATO, CHEDDAR, *and* CHIVE SOUP | LUMPY MASHED POTATOES

SWISS STEAK | CHICKEN *and* DUMPLINGS | TAMALE PIE

AMERICAN APPLE PIE SOUP | CHOCOLATE CHIP COOKIES

comes our love of beer brewing and drinking. Although beer has been brewed in America from the earliest colonial times, the art of brewing fine beers is experiencing a renaissance in America today.

In addition to fermented and distilled grains, fermented apple juice was an important part of the diet of early American settlers. Nearly every American homestead supported a few trees or, where possible, an entire orchard. Because many of those trees were seedlings, their fruit was often too bitter for eating out of hand, but just fine for brewing hard cider. Although harder to find in modern-day America, colder climates still produce both uncarbonated apple wines and hard ciders.

But the drink that has gained the most prominence is wine. Grapes were planted wherever immigrants from Mediterranean cultures settled. And where there were grapes, there was wine. But while European regional cuisines and wines grew up hand in hand, evolving so closely that the dishes of any given region were generally the most perfect match for its wines, and vice versa, from the early years of commercial wine making in America, our wines were made to an international model and measured against a French yardstick, with little appreciation for American regionality.

When choosing American wines to pair with traditional American dishes, therefore, what matters is personal taste. Wine is now produced in all fifty states (even Alaska). Which means you've got a whole continent of exploring to do.

BOSTON BAKED BEANS

Serves 4 to 6

Molasses from the West Indies was first shipped to Boston in the late seventeenth century, when it was used to replace maple sugar in the local dish of baked beans. Some versions of this classic dish also include brown sugar, tomato paste, ketchup, or maple syrup. In her 1896 Boston Cooking-School Cook Book, *Fannie Farmer says the addition of dry mustard was thought to make the beans more digestible. Though the recipe calls for an initial cooking of the beans, all the ingredients could easily be started together and cooked straight through for 8 hours.*

Rinse and sort through the beans. Place them in the slow cooker and add enough of the water to cover. Cover and cook on high for 2 hours, or until just tender. Or, soak the beans overnight in water to cover, then drain, rinse, and transfer to the slow cooker. Add the water to cover.

Add the onion, bacon, molasses, maple syrup, cloves, ginger, and dry mustard to the slow cooker. Cover and cook on low for 6 to 8 hours, until the beans are very tender. Stir in the salt just before serving. (You may wish to place the lid slightly ajar for the last 30 minutes of cooking time to concentrate any liquid and allow the top to caramelize.)

Transfer to a serving dish and serve immediately.

TO DRINK Though wines were imported in colonial times, hard cider was the drink of the farm family. Bill Rhyne in Sonoma County, California, produces a delicate and delightful hard cider, a historically appropriate choice for accompanying a bowl of Boston baked beans.

2 cups dried great Northern or navy beans

6 cups water or chicken stock (page 101)

1/2 yellow onion, finely chopped

2 strips thick hickory-smoked bacon, finely chopped

1/2 cup dark molasses

1/2 cup maple syrup

Pinch of ground cloves

Pinch of ground ginger

1 teaspoon dry mustard

2 teaspoons salt

RED BEANS *and* RICE

Serves 4 to 6

Reds beans and rice is a Louisiana favorite, traditionally served on Monday for lunch, using the ham bone left over from Sunday's ham dinner. Although ham hocks are traditional, this lower-fat version uses smoked pork chops. As with the Boston Baked Beans, you could skip the initial bean-cooking step and simply cook all the ingredients together for 8 hours.

Rinse and sort through the beans. Place them in the slow cooker and add enough of the water to cover. Cover and cook on high for 2 hours, or until just tender. Or, soak the beans overnight in water to cover, then drain, rinse, and transfer to the slow cooker. Add the water to cover.

Add the pork chop(s), celery, onion, bell pepper, bay leaves, thyme, oregano, garlic, cayenne, Tabasco, and sausages to the slow cooker. Cover and cook on low for 6 hours, until the beans are very tender and the pork chops are falling apart. Remove and discard the pork chop bones and break up any large chunks of meat with a fork. Remove and discard the bay leaves, thyme, and oregano.

Divide the rice among shallow bowls. Spoon the beans over the rice, dividing the meat evenly, and serve immediately.

TO DRINK Nothing but beer will do, perhaps a dark Munich lager. If beer's not your choice, a very gutsy dark red wine could substitute.

2 cups dried red beans

6 to 8 cups water

1 or 2 smoked pork chops

3 celery stalks, finely chopped

1 yellow onion, finely chopped

1 green bell pepper, finely chopped

2 bay leaves

3 sprigs thyme

3 sprigs oregano

1 tablespoon chopped fresh garlic

$1/2$ teaspoon ground cayenne pepper or crushed red pepper flakes

1 tablespoon Tabasco sauce

1 pound andouille sausages, diagonally sliced

4 to 6 cups cooked white rice

Potato, Cheddar, *and* Chive Soup

Serves 4 to 6

The combination of potatoes and cheese just can't be beat, especially here, in this rich, filling soup.

Place the potatoes and 1 cup of the stock in the slow cooker. Cover and cook on high for 2 hours, or until the potatoes are just tender.

Transfer two-thirds of the potatoes to a food processor or blender, along with the cooking liquid. Add the garlic. Blend to the desired consistency: a blender will yield a smooth texture, a food processor a rough, rustic consistency.

Return the potato purée to the slow cooker and stir in the shredded cheese, the remaining ⅔ cup stock, and the chives. Cover and cook on low for 30 minutes, or until the soup is well heated. Add extra stock or water if the soup is too thick. Break up the whole potato slices with a fork to achieve a texture that suits you. Season with salt and pepper. Stir in the cream just before serving.

Ladle into soup bowls, sprinkle with the crumbled cheese, and serve immediately.

SOUTHWESTERN POTATO-CHEDDAR SOUP

For a Southwestern version of this soup, use cilantro instead of chives, and add 1 (4-ounce) can chopped roasted green chiles and 1 teaspoon each ground cumin and coriander.

TO DRINK Mount Palomar Winery in Temecula, California, is currently the only United States winery to make wine from the Cortese grape. In northern Italy, the grape is used to make a wine called Gavi di Gavi. It's a lovely, smooth, relatively light-bodied, crisp white wine that goes well with either version of this soup.

6 large potatoes, peeled and sliced

1⅔ cups chicken stock, plus more as needed (page 101)

1 large clove garlic

1 cup shredded sharp Cheddar cheese, or a mixture of sharp Cheddar and smoked Gouda

¼ cup chopped fresh chives

Salt and freshly ground black pepper

1 cup heavy cream, half-and-half, or sour cream (optional)

¼ cup crumbled sharp Cheddar cheese, for garnish

Lumpy Mashed Potatoes

Serves 4 to 6

If you belong to the creamy–smooth mashed potatoes club, then this recipe is not for you. This is for those of us who like some substance and chew to our spuds. The slow cooker is great for mashed potatoes as you don't have to watch the time too closely or worry about overcooking.

Place the potatoes in the slow cooker and add the stock. Cover and cook on high for 2 hours, or until the potatoes are tender.

Using a potato masher, lightly mash the potatoes in the slow cooker, still leaving them fairly chunky. Gradually add the milk while mashing, until all of the milk has been incorporated into the potatoes. Continue to mash and blend until the potatoes are a consistency that suits you. Add salt and pepper to taste and mix well.

Transfer to a serving dish and serve at once.

TO DRINK Pair with whatever you're drinking with the main course.

4 to 6 large russet potatoes, peeled and cut into chunks

$1^1/_2$ cups chicken stock (page 101)

1 cup milk or half-and-half, heated

Salt and freshly ground black pepper

Swiss Steak

Serves 4 to 6

Swiss steak isn't Swiss at all, but an old American favorite, the first recipe for which appeared in print in 1915, according to food historian Jean Anderson. Its closest relative appears to be something called "smothered steak" in England. Since Swiss steak was often tenderized with a mallet before being added to the pot, the name may have come from the English term "swissing," a method of smoothing out cloth between a set of rollers. Swiss steak should be served over a mound of mashed potatoes.

Combine the flour, salt, and several pinches of pepper in a resealable plastic bag. Add the meat to the bag, several pieces at a time, and shake to coat completely.

Heat a large sauté pan over medium-high heat and add the oil. In batches if necessary, add the meat and cook, turning, for 7 to 10 minutes, until browned on both sides. Using tongs, transfer the meat to the slow cooker.

Add the onion to the remaining flour in the bag and shake to coat. Set the sauté pan over medium-high heat and add the onion. Sauté, stirring frequently, for about 10 minutes, until lightly browned. Gradually add the water, stirring to scrape up the browned bits from the bottom of the pan. Cook, stirring frequently, for 10 to 15 minutes, until the sauce thickens enough to lightly coat the back of a spoon. Pour over the meat in the slow cooker. Sprinkle the carrots over the top.

Cover and cook on low for 6 to 8 hours, until the meat is very tender. Divide the meat and sauce among dinner plates and serve immediately.

TO DRINK A light- to medium-bodied Oregon Pinot Noir.

1 cup all-purpose flour

2 teaspoons salt

Freshly ground black pepper

2 pounds beef round, sirloin, or skirt steak, trimmed of fat and cut into 1-inch slices

2 tablespoons vegetable oil

1 yellow onion, halved and sliced

2 cups water

3 carrots, peeled and cut into 1-inch chunks (optional)

CHICKEN *and* DUMPLINGS

Serves 4 to 6

Recipes for chicken and dumplings were brought to this country by French, German, British, and eastern European immigrants, just to name a few. And variations can be found among the Pennsylvania Dutch and in the Deep South, the Midwest, and New England. This particular recipe is my mother's, passed down from her mother, the daughter of Irish immigrants.

Combine the flour and salt in a resealable plastic bag. Add the chicken to the bag, several pieces at a time, and shake to coat completely.

Heat a large sauté pan over medium-high heat and add 2 tablespoons of the oil. Add the chicken and cook, turning once, for 5 to 7 minutes, until browned on both sides. Using tongs, transfer to paper towels to drain, then place in the slow cooker.

Add the onion and celery to the remaining flour in the bag and shake to coat. Set the sauté pan over medium-high heat and add the remaining 1 tablespoon oil. Add the onion and celery and sauté, stirring frequently, for 10 to 15 minutes, until browned. Gradually add the stock, stirring to scrape up the browned bits from the bottom of the pan. Cook, stirring frequently, for 10 to 15 minutes, until the sauce is somewhat thickened. Stir in the carrots, marjoram, and salt and pepper to taste. Pour over the chicken in the slow cooker.

Cover and cook on low for 3½ hours, then on high for 30 minutes before dropping in the dumplings.

(continued)

1 cup all-purpose flour

2 teaspoons salt

1 frying or stewing chicken, cut into serving pieces and skinned

3 tablespoons vegetable oil

1 yellow onion, halved and sliced

1 celery stalk, sliced

2 cups chicken stock (page 101)

3 carrots, peeled and sliced

2 sprigs marjoram

Freshly ground black pepper

1 cup fresh or frozen peas

To prepare the dumplings, combine the flour, baking powder, and salt in a bowl. Stir to blend. Bring the butter and milk to a simmer in a saucepan over medium heat. Drizzle into the dry ingredients and mix well. This will be a fairly dry dough.

Using a large spoon or your hands, form the dough into 6 loose ovals or rounds, about 2 inches in diameter. Add the peas to the slow cooker and mix well. Place the dumplings on top of the stew.

Cover and cook on high for 30 minutes, or until a toothpick inserted in a dumpling comes out clean. Remove and discard the marjoram.

Spoon the stew into shallow bowls, dividing the chicken and dumplings evenly. Garnish with the parsley and serve immediately.

TO DRINK A great fit would be the medium-bodied Ca'del Solo Big House White from imaginative wine maker Randall Grahm, owner of Bonny Doon Vineyards in Santa Cruz, California. The wine is named for the vineyards its fruit comes from, close to one of California's state prisons. It's a blend of Sauvignon Blanc, Riesling, Pinot Blanc, and Viognier.

Dumplings

2 cups all-purpose flour

1 tablespoon baking powder

$3/4$ teaspoon salt

3 tablespoons unsalted butter

1 cup milk

$1/4$ cup chopped fresh parsley, for garnish

Tamale Pie

Serves 4 to 6

Although the tamale is a traditional Mexican food, tamale pie is a purely American invention that is much less time-consuming to make than tamales. With tamale pie, it's easy to feed a crew with little effort.

To prepare the filling, place the cumin in a mortar or coffee grinder and grind to a coarse powder.

Heat a large sauté pan over medium-high heat. Add the meat and onion and cook, stirring frequently to break up the meat, for 7 to 10 minutes, until browned. Stir in the cumin, bell pepper, chili powder, and cornmeal and cook for 3 to 4 minutes, until the bell pepper is softened. Stir in the tomatoes, chili sauce, corn, and olives. Add the cheese and stir until melted. Add salt to taste and stir well.

Pour the filling into the slow cooker. Cover and cook on low for 2 to 3 hours, until the meat is cooked and heated through.

To prepare the crust, combine the cornmeal, flour, sugar, baking powder, and baking soda in a bowl and stir to mix well. In a separate bowl, combine the oil, eggs, and buttermilk. Whisk to blend. Add the wet ingredients to the dry ingredients and stir just until blended.

Spread the batter on top of the filling in the slow cooker. Leaving the lid slightly ajar, cook on high for 1 hour, or until a toothpick inserted into the crust comes out dry.

Spoon the pie onto dinner plates and serve immediately.

TO DRINK Neibaum-Coppola's Francis Coppola Rosso, a California red table wine blend of Zinfandel, Syrah, Cabernet, and Sangiovese.

Filling

1 tablespoon cumin seed

2 pounds lean ground beef

1 yellow onion, finely chopped

$1/2$ green bell pepper, finely chopped

2 tablespoons chili powder

2 tablespoons cornmeal

1 ($14^1/2$-ounce) can crushed tomatoes

$1/4$ cup Heinz chili sauce

1 cup fresh or frozen corn kernels

1 cup canned pitted black olives, halved

1 cup shredded sharp Cheddar cheese

Salt

Crust

1 cup cornmeal

1 cup all-purpose flour

$1/4$ cup sugar

$1^1/2$ teaspoons baking powder

$1/2$ teaspoon baking soda

2 tablespoons vegetable oil

2 eggs

1 cup buttermilk

AMERICAN APPLE PIE SOUP

Serves 4 to 6

Apples have been in this country as long as European settlers have. Although apples have traditionally been made into pies, juice, cider, butters, and sauce and baked whole, here they are used to make a spicy dessert soup. The soup is versatile enough that it can also be served as a main course, accompanied by fresh Cheddar cheese biscuits.

Combine the cinnamon, cloves, and allspice in a mortar or coffee grinder and grind to a fine powder.

Combine the water, apples, raisins, nutmeg, and spice mixture in the slow cooker. Cover and cook on low for 4 to 6 hours, until the apples are quite soft and falling apart.

Just before serving, stir in the lemon juice, brandy, and honey to taste. Ladle into soup bowls and top with a dollop of yogurt. Serve immediately.

TO DRINK Rhyne Hard Cyder, a light Sauvignon Blanc, or even an American apple wine, such as Carlos Creek Winery's Apple Ice Wine.

1 cinnamon stick, broken into pieces

6 whole cloves

6 allspice berries

6 cups water or apple cider

4 large Granny Smith apples, cored and sliced

$^2/_3$ cup raisins

1 teaspoon ground nutmeg

2 tablespoons freshly squeezed lemon juice

2 tablespoons brandy (optional)

3 to 4 tablespoons honey (optional)

$^1/_2$ cup yogurt or sour cream, for serving

CHOCOLATE CHIP COOKIES

Serves 6 to 8

Who would have thought you could make chocolate chip cookies in a slow cooker? Though they'll certainly look different from what you're used to, the flavor is great and they're easier and less labor-intensive to make. The cookie slices are delicious topped with ice cream, or simply served with a tall glass of cold milk.

Grease the slow cooker insert with butter or vegetable oil. Cut a piece of waxed paper to fit the bottom and grease the waxed paper.

In a bowl, beat the butter, eggs, sugars, and vanilla together until light and fluffy. In a separate bowl, stir the flour, baking soda, and salt together. Stir the dry ingredients into the butter mixture. Stir in the chocolate chips and walnuts until well blended.

Spoon the dough evenly into the slow cooker and smooth the top. Cover and cook on low for about 3 hours, until a toothpick inserted into the center comes out clean. Set the lid slightly ajar for the last 30 minutes.

Turn off the heat and remove the insert from the slow cooker. Allow to cool in the insert for 30 minutes. Invert onto a wire rack. Cut the cake in half lengthwise, then cut each piece crosswise into slices. Serve warm or at room temperature.

TO DRINK Milk is the only proper accompaniment for chocolate chip cookies.

1 cup unsalted butter, at room temperature

2 eggs

$^1/_2$ cup firmly packed brown sugar

$^1/_2$ cup granulated sugar

1 tablespoon pure vanilla extract

2 cups all-purpose flour

$^1/_2$ teaspoon baking soda

$^1/_4$ teaspoon salt

1 cup semisweet chocolate chips

1 cup coarsely chopped walnuts

Mexico

Earthenware casseroles are still widely used in Mexico today. Commonly, they fall into two general categories: the *cazuela,* a wide bowl used for cooking soups or stews, and the *olla,* a tall pot with a narrow neck, usually used for cooking beans. There are also large *comals*, used for cooking tortillas and toasting spices. Many traditional Mexican cooks believe these earthenware vessels impart a unique earthy flavor to foods.

These vessels are crafted for use either in the oven or over direct heat. The indigenous peoples of Mexico and the southwestern United States traditionally cooked over an open fire. *Hornos,* or adobe ovens, were brought to the region by Europeans.

Beans, stews, soups . . . all those dishes that require the long, slow application of heat are often still cooked on top of the stove or over an open fire in rural Mexico. And the earthenware casseroles in which to cook them can be found in markets all over the country. Although the shapes tend to remain uniform, the colors and textures vary from region to region, depending on the earth from which the vessels were made. Needless to say, it is these bean, stew, and soup dishes that are most adaptable for use in the slow cooker.

Mexican Food and Drink

For most Americans, pairing beer with Mexican food is about as natural as pairing milk with cookies. And most Mexicans today are likely to agree.

Before the arrival of the first Europeans, Mexico's native people drank chocolate and pulque (fermented agave). But with the arrival of the Europeans, things changed. The conquistadors and

CHICKEN MOLE | PORK STEW *in* TOMATILLO SAUCE | REFRIED BEANS

STUFFED-CHILE CASSEROLE *with* RED *and* GREEN SALSAS

CHICKEN *in* PEANUT *and* CHILE SAUCE

SPICED MEATBALLS *in* CHIPOTLE SAUCE

missionaries brought European grapevine cuttings for planting in the New World. From Mexico, vine plantings spread throughout the Americas.

But in 1594, King Phillip II of Spain forbade new vine plantings in Mexico. He acted in response to complaints from Spanish wine makers whose export business was being affected by the growing number of wines produced in the New World. As a result, old vineyards were torn out and no new ones were planted. The choice for Mexicans was clear: drink imported Spanish wines or drink something else.

It was only in the early years of the twentieth century that wine making began to experience a renaissance in Mexico. Today, the center of Mexico's fine-wine industry is in Baja California's Valle de Guadalupe, an hour and a half by car from San Diego.

When pairing wines with Mexican foods, remember that tannins accentuate the heat found in chiles, so lighter, fruitier-style red wines that are lower in tannins work better with strong Mexican flavors. White wines with plenty of acid and fruit also work well. For this reason, some restaurateurs are now choosing acidic Greek, Spanish, and Italian white wines for Mexican foods. Sparkling wines, such as blanc de blancs, blanc de noirs, and the new crop of red sparkling wines (such as sparkling Shiraz from Australia) also complement Mexican foods.

CHICKEN MOLE

Serves 4 to 6

According to legend, this dish was created by nuns in a convent in Puebla. It's a skillful combination of Old World flavors (chicken, raisins, almonds, and spices) with those of the New (chiles, chocolate, and tomatoes). In Mexico, mole is a dish for special celebrations. It can take many hours or even days to make properly, and its preparation is usually a communal activity. In a traditional kitchen, the ingredients for mole are ground by hand on a metate, a lava rock mortar. Although I have taken liberties with the traditional preparation methods, the recipe is still somewhat time-consuming, however, the results are well worth the effort. Serve with rice.

Preheat the oven to 350°F. Combine the almonds, cinnamon, coriander, aniseed, sesame seed, and cloves on a baking sheet. Place in the oven and toast for 10 minutes, or until fragrant and lightly browned. Remove from the oven and set aside.

Spread all the chiles on a separate baking sheet and toast at 350°F for 10 minutes, or until the chiles puff up but do not darken; take care not to burn them. Remove from the oven and let cool slightly. Tear into flat pieces and place in a bowl. Pour 2 cups of the chicken stock over the chiles and allow to soak for about 1 hour.

Preheat the broiler. Place the tomato on a baking sheet and broil, turning, for 5 to 7 minutes, until blackened on all sides. Remove from the oven and allow to cool. Peel when cool enough to handle.

1/4 cup blanched almonds

1 cinnamon stick, broken into pieces

1/2 teaspoon coriander seed

1/2 teaspoon aniseed

1/4 cup sesame seed

4 whole cloves

4 mulato chiles, stemmed and seeded

4 ancho chiles, stemmed and seeded

4 pasilla chiles, stemmed and seeded

4 cups chicken stock (page 101)

Place the chiles and their stock in a blender and purée until very smooth. In batches, add the toasted almonds and spices, tomato, chocolate, garlic, onion, raisins, and salt to taste and blend until smooth, adding the remaining 2 cups stock as needed to make the consistency you prefer. The sauce should be just thick enough to coat the back of a spoon. If you want a smooth sauce, strain it through a medium-meshed sieve to remove the seeds and pieces of chile.

Arrange the chicken in the slow cooker and carefully pour the sauce over. Cover and cook on low for 3 to 8 hours, until the chicken is tender. At 3 to 4 hours, the chicken will still be firm and hold its shape. At 6 to 8 hours, the meat will be falling off the bone. Transfer to dinner plates and serve immediately.

TO DRINK Château Camou's Flor de Guadalupe Zinfandel, a light, fruity Zin, or you could try a heavier Bordeaux blend.

1 large tomato

3 ounces Mexican or semisweet chocolate, chopped, or $^1/_3$ cup unsweetened cocoa powder

5 cloves garlic

1 white onion, coarsely chopped

$^1/_4$ cup raisins

Salt

1 chicken, cut into serving pieces and skinned

Pork Stew *in* Tomatillo Sauce

Serves 4 to 6

This simple stew is best served over rice. The longer you cook it, the more tender the pork will become. If you prefer a thicker texture, add another corn tortilla. The variation that follows is for an even simpler version.

Preheat the broiler. Place the tomatillos, chiles, onion, and garlic on a baking sheet. Broil, turning occasionally, for 5 to 7 minutes, until blackened. Remove from the broiler and transfer to a cutting board. When cool enough to handle, chop the vegetables.

Transfer the vegetables to a blender and add the tortilla, stock, and fennel. Purée until almost smooth. Add more stock as needed to achieve the thickness you prefer.

Heat a large sauté pan over medium-high heat and add the oil. In batches if necessary, add the pork and cook, turning, for 8 to 10 minutes, until browned on all sides. Using tongs, transfer to the slow cooker.

Pour the sauce over the pork. Cover and cook on low for 6 to 8 hours, until the meat is very tender. Stir in the cilantro and salt to taste about 10 minutes before serving.

Transfer to a serving dish and sprinkle the cheese over the top. Serve immediately.

(continued)

3 pounds tomatillos, husked and rinsed

6 to 8 serrano chiles, stemmed and seeded

1 white onion, chopped

2 cloves garlic, minced

1 corn tortilla, chopped

2 cups chicken stock, plus more as needed (page 101)

Pinch of ground fennel

3 tablespoons vegetable oil

2^1/$_2$ pounds lean pork stew meat, cut into 1^1/$_2$-inch cubes

2 tablespoons chopped cilantro

Salt

4 ounces Mexican queso fresco or feta cheese, crumbled (1 scant cup)

EASY PORK STEW IN CHILE VERDE

Heat a sauté pan over medium-high heat and add the oil. In batches if necessary, add the pork and cook, turning, for 8 to 10 minutes, until browned on all sides. Using tongs, transfer to the slow cooker and add the chile sauce and salsa. Mix well. Cover and cook on low for 6 to 8 hours, until the meat is tender. Serve garnished with chopped cilantro.

TO DRINK Beer would be a good choice. Or try Monte Xanic's aromatic medium-bodied Viña Kristel, a Bordeaux blend of Sauvignon Blanc and Semillon; or Château Camou's medium-bodied Blanc de Blanc, a blend of Chenin Blanc, Sauvignon Blanc, and Chardonnay.

Easy Pork Stew in Chile Verde

3 tablespoons vegetable oil

2 pounds lean pork stew meat, cut into $1^1/_2$-inch cubes

1 (32-ounce) can green chile sauce

1 (16-ounce) jar chunky green chile salsa

$^1/_4$ cup chopped cilantro, for garnish

Refried Beans

Serves 4 to 6, with leftovers

More than any other food, beans are the most traditional Mexican one-pot meal. A staple of life in the Americas for thousands of years, beans have traditionally been slow cooked in an earthenware bean pot called an olla *over an open fire. They are still cooked that way in rural Mexican homes. Mexican beans are usually embellished with little more than a bit of salt and some onion, leaving the beans to show off their own unique flavors. I have added a few spices to the dish, but they are optional.*

Black beans are more typical of southern Mexican dishes, while pinto and pink beans are traditional in northern Mexico.

Preheat the broiler. Place the onion, garlic, and chiles on a baking sheet and broil, turning, for 5 to 7 minutes, until blackened and blistered on all sides. Remove from the broiler and transfer to a cutting board. Chop coarsely.

Combine the cumin and coriander in a mortar or coffee grinder and grind to a coarse powder.

Rinse and sort through the beans. Place in the slow cooker and add the water and beer. Add the onion mixture and the spice mixture and stir well. Cover and cook on low for 8 hours, or until the beans are very tender.

Heat a large sauté pan over medium-high heat and add the oil. Spoon the beans into the pan, a bit at a time, and smash them with a potato masher. Gradually add all the beans, then any remaining liquid, and cook until some of the liquid evaporates and the beans thicken. The finished beans should have some texture to them. (If you want a smoother texture, purée them in a food processor before transferring to the sauté pan.) Stir in salt to taste and serve warm.

TO DRINK For these beans, it's beer: Moctezuma's Noche Buena or Dos Equis.

1 white onion, quartered

6 cloves garlic

4 serrano chiles, seeded and halved

1 tablespoon cumin seed (optional)

1 tablespoon coriander seed (optional)

2 cups dried pinto or black beans

4 cups water

2 cups beer

3 to 4 tablespoons vegetable oil

Salt

STUFFED-CHILE CASSEROLE
with RED *and* GREEN SALSAS

Serves 4 to 6

In Mexico, stuffed chiles are usually filled with meat, cheese, or rice; fried in a batter; and served with red or green sauce. Here, the chiles are stuffed with a mélange of three cheeses, baked in a soufflé-like mixture, and topped with both red and green salsas for a dish that is colorful and delicious.

To prepare the orange and chile salsa, preheat the oven to 350°F. Place the chiles on a baking sheet and roast for 10 minutes, or until puffed; be careful not to burn them. Remove from the oven and allow to cool. Remove the stems and seeds and tear the chiles into flat pieces. Place in a bowl, pour in the orange juice, and soak for 30 minutes, or until softened.

Using a garlic press, press the garlic into the chile mixture, then transfer to a blender. Purée until smooth, adding more orange juice if necessary to achieve the consistency you prefer. Stir in salt to taste.

To prepare the salsa verde, bring the water to a boil in a saucepan over high heat. Add the tomatillos, 4 of the garlic cloves, the onion, and chiles. Cook for 15 minutes, or until the tomatillos are soft. Remove from the heat and allow to cool. Drain in a colander placed over a bowl, reserving the cooking water.

In a blender, combine the tomatillo mixture with 1 cup of the reserved cooking water, the remaining 3 garlic cloves, the cilantro, and salt to taste. Purée until smooth, adding more of the reserved water if needed to achieve the consistency you prefer.

(continued)

Orange Juice and Chile Salsa

8 pasilla, ancho, or dried New Mexico chiles

2 cups freshly squeezed orange juice, plus more as needed

4 to 6 cloves garlic

Salt

Salsa Verde

4 cups water

12 tomatillos, husked and rinsed

7 cloves garlic

3 tablespoons coarsely chopped white onion

4 to 8 serrano chiles, stemmed

3/4 cup cilantro leaves

Salt

Preheat the oven to 500°F. Cover a baking sheet with aluminum foil.

Place the chiles on the baking sheet and roast, turning occasionally, for about 20 minutes, until blackened and puffed on all sides. Remove from the oven and cover with a damp kitchen towel for about 10 minutes.

Meanwhile, combine the jack, goat, and feta cheeses in a bowl and mix well.

Gently scrape the skins off the chiles. Cut off the stem ends and remove the seeds, being careful to keep the chiles in one piece. Stuff the chiles with the cheese mixture and set aside on a plate.

Oil the slow cooker and preheat on high for 5 to 10 minutes. (This will help the egg mixture puff.)

Place the egg whites in a large bowl and beat with an electric mixer on high speed until soft peaks form. Place the egg yolks and beer in a separate bowl and whisk until smooth. Stir in the salt. Slowly and carefully fold the yolk mixture into the whites.

Lay the stuffed chiles in the slow cooker and pour the egg mixture over them. Cover and cook on high for 1½ to 2 hours, until the eggs are puffed and lightly browned. To help with the browning, place the lid slightly ajar for the last 20 minutes of cooking.

Divide the chiles among dinner plates and spoon some of the red chile salsa and some of the salsa verde over each. Serve immediately.

TO DRINK Monte Xanic's crisp, light, dry Reserve Chenin Blanc or Château Camou's El Gran Vino Blanco, a rich, fruity Sauvignon Blanc.

6 to 8 large poblano or fresh Anaheim chiles

1 cup shredded Monterey jack cheese

10 ounces goat cheese

4 ounces feta cheese, grated or crumbled (1 scant cup)

6 eggs, separated

1/2 cup beer

1/2 teaspoon salt

CHICKEN *in* PEANUT *and* CHILE SAUCE

Serves 4 to 6

Like so many other Mexican dishes, this one incorporates ingredients from both the Old World and the New. It's an amazingly rich and spicy dish, and one of my all-time favorites. The chipotle chiles in adobo sauce are available in most supermarkets. Ancho chiles are dried poblanos and can be found in Latin American markets or obtained from such mail-order companies as Melissa's Produce (see resources).

Tear the ancho chiles into flat pieces and place in a small bowl. Add 1 cup of the stock and soak for 30 minutes to rehydrate.

Combine the peppercorns, allspice, cinnamon, and cloves in a mortar or coffee grinder and grind to a coarse powder.

If using fresh tomatoes, preheat the broiler. Place the tomatoes on a baking sheet and broil, turning, for 5 to 7 minutes, until blackened on all sides. Remove from the oven and allow to cool. Peel when cool enough to handle.

Heat a sauté pan over medium-high heat and add the oil. Add the onion and garlic and sauté, stirring frequently, for 10 to 15 minutes, until browned.

Transfer the tomatoes and the onion mixture to a blender and add the ancho chiles and their stock, the spice mixture, the remaining 2 cups stock, the peanuts, bread, and chipotle chiles. Purée until smooth.

Place the chicken in the slow cooker, add the sauce, and toss well. Cover and cook on low for 3 to 8 hours, until the chicken is tender. At 3 to 4 hours, the chicken will still be firm and hold its shape. At 6 to 8 hours, the meat will be falling off the bone. Season with salt to taste. Transfer to a serving dish and serve immediately.

TO DRINK L. A. Cetto's full, rich Private Reserve Chardonnay or Monte Xanic's lighter-bodied Calixa Blanco.

2 ancho chiles, stemmed and seeded

3 cups chicken stock (page 101)

6 peppercorns

6 allspice berries

1 cinnamon stick, broken into pieces

6 whole cloves

2 large tomatoes, or 1 (14^1/$_2$-ounce) can crushed tomatoes

3 tablespoons peanut or vegetable oil

^{1}/$_2$ white onion, sliced

2 cloves garlic, chopped

1^1/$_4$ cups unsalted dry-roasted peanuts

1 slice stale white or French bread, torn into small pieces

2 canned chipotle chiles in adobo sauce

1 chicken, cut into serving pieces and skinned

Salt

SPICED MEATBALLS *in* CHIPOTLE CHILE SAUCE

Serves 4 to 6

These albóndigas *("meatballs" in Spanish) are served in tomato-chipotle sauce, and should be accompanied by rice. This particular recipe was inspired by that maven of Mexican cooking, Diana Kennedy. You can regulate the amount of heat in the sauce by the number of chipotle chiles you use.*

To prepare the sauce, combine the cumin, coriander, garlic, oregano leaves, and thyme leaves in a mortar or coffee grinder and grind to a coarse consistency.

Heat a dry large sauté pan over high heat. Tear the dried chile into several large pieces and place in the pan. Toast for 3 minutes, or until puffed but not browned. Transfer to a bowl and add the tomatoes.

Heat the sauté pan over medium-high heat and add the oil. Add the onion and sauté, stirring frequently, for 10 minutes, or until lightly browned. Add the spice mixture and stir for 2 to 3 minutes.

Transfer to a blender or food processor and add the chile mixture, chipotle chiles, and salt to taste. Purée until smooth, adding the stock as necessary to thin the sauce.

Pour the sauce into the slow cooker. Cover and cook on low while you prepare the meatballs.

Sauce

1 teaspoon cumin seed

1 teaspoon coriander seed

3 cloves garlic

Leaves from 2 sprigs oregano

Leaves from 1 sprig thyme

1 dried New Mexico or pasilla chile, stemmed and seeded

1 (28-ounce) can crushed tomatoes

1 tablespoon vegetable oil

1 white onion, thinly sliced

2 canned chipotle chiles in adobo sauce (or more, if you prefer a hotter sauce)

Salt

1 cup chicken stock (page 101) or water

To prepare the meatballs, combine the peppercorns, allspice, cumin, coriander, and oregano in a mortar or coffee grinder and grind to a fine powder.

Place the meat in a large bowl, add the egg, and mix well. Add the spice mixture, salt, onion, garlic, and crackers and mix well. Using your hands, form the meat into 2-inch balls.

Heat a large sauté pan over medium-high heat and add the oil. Add the meatballs and cook, turning, for 6 to 8 minutes, until browned on the outside but still rare on the inside.

Add the meatballs to the sauce in the slow cooker. Cover and cook on low for 2 to 8 hours, until the meatballs are cooked through. At 2 to 3 hours, the meatballs will still hold their shape. At 6 to 8 hours, the meatballs will have fallen apart into the sauce. Transfer to a serving dish and serve immediately.

TO DRINK The very soft, fruity Barbera from Bodega Santo Tomas makes a good pairing with this dish. Also, microbreweries are taking off in Mexico these days, just as they are in the United States. Try something from Cerveza Casta in Apodaca or Sierra Madre Brewing in Monterrey.

Meatballs

8 peppercorns

4 allspice berries

1 teaspoon cumin seed

1 teaspoon coriander seed

Leaves from 2 sprigs oregano

1 1/2 pounds lean ground beef or pork

1 egg

2 teaspoons salt

1/2 white onion, finely chopped

3 cloves garlic, minced

8 soda crackers, crumbled

1 tablespoon vegetable oil

Great Britain

Although the British Isles encompass three distinct countries, each with its own separate cultures and traditions, England, Ireland, and Scotland occupy the same northern European island climate.

For at least ten centuries, the mainstay of the cooking of the British Isles has been its cereal and dairy products. Barley, oats, and rye grow readily in the cold and damp, so bread or some type of gruel formed the basis of the common man's diet. A strong tradition of dairying and cheese making also exists in Britain, with some of the finest examples of British farmhouse cheeses now being imported to the United States by Neal's Yard Dairy, a company founded to keep British cheese-making traditions alive.

Root vegetables, most notably carrots and potatoes, and cold-weather crops, such as broccoli, cabbage, cauliflower, and Brussels sprouts, also make up an important part of British cooking. When it comes to fruits, Britain does not have the right climate for most stone fruits, thus fruit offerings tend to run toward apples, quinces, pears, and berries.

Meats, as in most other rural economies, have traditionally been reserved for special occasions. Certainly wild game has always played an important role in the British Isles, but, as elsewhere, the choicest hunting grounds were often protected for the exclusive use of nobles.

One of the earliest methods of cooking meat was in a boiling pit: a large hole dug in the ground, lined with stones, and filled with water. Additional stones were heated in a nearby fire, then dropped into the pit to heat the water. The meat would actually be cooked in this boiling water.

One-pot meals were often cooked in three-legged metal cauldrons set over a hearth. Earthenware pots were also used. Traditional stews include

CORNED BEEF *and* CABBAGE | BEEF *and* GUINNESS STEW

IRISH CHEESE PUDDING | SCOTCH BROTH | DUBLIN CODDLE

OATMEAL SOUP | IRISH CHAMP

combinations of meats and root vegetables, slow cooked for warm, hearty flavors, and usually served with a hunk of good bread.

British Food and Drink

Although there is a long-standing tradition of home wine making in Britain, and a small but growing wine industry in southern England, fermented and distilled grain beverages have long been favored by the inhabitants of the British Isles.

The obvious reason for the lack of a well-developed wine industry is that grapes don't ripen well in the cold, damp climate of northern Europe. Grains such as wheat, rye, barley, and oats, on the other hand, do. In addition, hops, used to add an extra dimension of flavor to fermented grain beverages, grow easily in this climate.

So although there are plenty of wines that pair well with British dishes, and although Britain itself has long been one of the most profitable markets for European wines, rural British Isles fare is more traditionally served with beer. For this reason, I've drawn mainly from the British and northern European beer-brewing traditions for pairing with the dishes in this chapter.

All good beers exhibit the sweet flavor of malted grain and the slight bitterness of hops. Beyond that, though beers may range widely in style and flavor, most will pair well with slow-cooked foods. Ales, for instance, often have a slight fruitiness from the yeasts used in fermenting. Porters and stouts may have chocolate or coffee flavors from the roasted malts used in the brewing process. And wheat beers are refreshing and tart.

CORNED BEEF *and* CABBAGE

Serves 6

Corned beef and cabbage is a traditional Easter Sunday dinner in Ireland, and a St. Patrick's Day favorite for many Americans. Cabbage, potatoes, and carrots are common during the colder months in the British Isles since they store well. Corned beef and cabbage should be served with a crock of mustard. (See my book Lost Arts *for homemade mustard recipes.)*

In the slow cooker, combine the beef, carrots, potatoes, onions, cabbage, thyme, and bay leaf. Add the water and beer.

Cover and cook on low for 8 to 10 hours, until the meat and vegetables are very tender. Remove and discard the thyme and bay leaf.

Transfer the beef to a cutting board and cut into thin slices. Divide the meat among shallow bowls, surround with the vegetables, and spoon some of the cooking liquid over the top. Serve immediately.

TO DRINK Guinness stout or Harp Lager (brewed by Guinness according to a traditional Irish recipe).

3 pounds corned beef

3 large carrots, peeled and cut into bite-sized pieces

3 large potatoes, peeled and cut into bite-sized pieces

2 large yellow onions, quartered

1 green cabbage, cored and cut into 8 pieces

1 sprig thyme

1 bay leaf

2 cups water

1 cup Guinness stout or Harp Lager

BEEF *and* GUINNESS STEW

Serves 4 to 6

Root vegetables are always found in the cuisine of cold northern climates. In this delicious traditional Irish stew, beef is paired with carrots, onions, potatoes, and hearty Guinness stout. For a completely different flavor using basically the same ingredients, try using lamb shanks rather than beef. Both are Irish favorites.

Place the flour in a resealable plastic bag. Add the beef to the bag, several pieces at a time, and shake to coat completely.

Heat a large sauté pan over medium-high heat and add the oil. In batches if necessary, add the beef and cook, turning, for 8 to 10 minutes, until browned on all sides. Using tongs, transfer to paper towels to drain.

Place the beef, potatoes, carrots, onions, and thyme in the slow cooker and pour the beer over the top. (If you prefer the vegetables with more texture, let the stew cook for 1 hour before adding the vegetables.) Cover and cook on low for 8 hours, or until the meat is very tender. Season with salt. Remove and discard the thyme.

Transfer to a serving bowl and garnish generously with the parsley.

^{3}/4 cup all-purpose flour

2^1/2 pounds very lean stewing
beef, cut into 1^1/2-inch cubes

2 tablespoons vegetable oil

2 to 3 large potatoes, peeled and
cut into bite-sized pieces

2 to 3 carrots, peeled and cut into
bite-sized pieces

2 large yellow onions, quartered

1 to 2 sprigs thyme

2 cups Guinness stout or other
very dark, hearty beer

1 teaspoon salt

Chopped fresh parsley, for
garnish

LAMB AND GUINNESS STEW

Trim off as much fat from 4 to 6 lamb shanks as you can. The shanks will still render plenty of fat during cooking. For a lower-fat dish, cook them in the Guinness with ½ onion all day, then refrigerate the stew overnight and remove the congealed fat before finishing the dish. Add the potatoes, carrots, onions, and thyme. Cover and cook on low for 2 to 3 hours before serving.

TO DRINK What else? A Guinness or a Harp, also made by Guinness but lighter. Either beer could be used to make the stew and to drink with it.

IRISH CHEESE PUDDING

Serves 4 to 6

The Irish have long had a rich variety of milk products: buttermilk, butter, curds, and cheeses made from goat's, sheep's, and cow's milk. As in other traditional dairying cultures around the world, cheese is a valued way of using up extra milk. This savory bread pudding would traditionally have been baked in an oven, yet it adapts well to the slow cooker.

The success of this dish depends upon the quality of its few ingredients: hearty dark beer, flavorful bread, and aged sharp Cheddar. Although not traditional, I love using a good sourdough bread in this recipe for additional bite. A dark beer or ale will darken the color of the finished pudding, but I prefer the rich flavor it adds to the dish.

Place the bread and 2½ cups of the cheese in the slow cooker and toss well.

In a bowl, combine the eggs, beer, half-and-half, cayenne, and mustard and whisk until frothy.

Pour the egg mixture over the bread, pressing down with the back of a spoon so that the bread absorbs some of the liquid. Cover and cook on low for about 3 hours, until the pudding is set. Sprinkle the remaining ½ cup cheese over the top 20 minutes before the end of cooking, leaving the lid slightly ajar so the top browns.

Spoon the pudding into bowls and garnish each serving with a sprinkle of parsley. Serve immediately.

TO DRINK A gutsy, tangy wheat beer from Widmer Brothers in Portland, Oregon, or from Anderson Valley Brewing Company in Boonville, California.

6 to 7 cups 1-inch cubes sourdough bread, with crust

3 cups shredded sharp Cheddar cheese

4 eggs

3 cups dark beer or chicken stock (page 101), or equal amounts of the two

1 cup half-and-half

Pinch of cayenne pepper

1 tablespoon hot sweet mustard

¼ cup chopped fresh parsley

SCOTCH BROTH

Serves 4 to 6

This dish is a Scotch tradition hundreds of years old. Not a broth in the sense we define it, the dish has plenty of substance: lamb stock, barley, carrots, and onions at the very least. In addition, some recipes contain celery, cabbage, and potatoes. It's a great way to use up any leftover Lamb and Guinness Stew.

In the slow cooker, combine the lamb, barley, carrot, leeks, celery, and water. Cover and cook on low for 6 to 8 hours, until the meat is very tender. Stir in salt and pepper to taste.

Transfer to bowls and garnish with the parsley. Serve immediately.

TO DRINK A Scotch beer or ale.

2 lamb shoulder chops, or 1 cup meat and broth from Lamb and Guinness Stew (page 41)

$^1/_3$ cup pearl barley

1 large carrot, peeled and cubed

2 leeks, white part only, cut into $^1/_2$-inch pieces

1 celery stalk, thickly sliced

6 cups water

Salt and freshly ground black pepper

$^1/_4$ cup chopped fresh parsley, for garnish

DUBLIN CODDLE

Serves 6

Dublin Coddle is true Irish comfort food: no fancy sauces, and none of the spices found in hotter regions. Yet every Dublin pub and every Dublin mum has a version of it. It sounds simple—just bacon, sausage, potatoes, onions, carrots, and water or hard cider—but the flavors meld together into a delicious stew.

Note: This dish is an exception to the better-the-day-after rule. I like it hot out of the pot.

Heat a large sauté pan over medium-high heat. Add the bacon and fry for 7 minutes, or until crisp. Using tongs, transfer to paper towels to drain.

Add the sausages to the pan and cook, turning frequently, for 10 minutes, or until browned. Using tongs, transfer to a plate. Drain any excess fat from the pan.

Add the onions to the pan and sauté, stirring frequently, for 10 minutes, or until lightly browned.

Spread half of the onions in a layer in the bottom of the slow cooker. Sprinkle with salt and pepper. Place half of the potatoes in a layer on top of the onions and sprinkle with salt and pepper. Lay the strips of bacon over the potatoes. Lay the sausages over the bacon. Spread the carrots over the sausages and sprinkle with salt and pepper. Spread the remaining onions over the carrots and sprinkle with salt and pepper. Top with the remaining potatoes and sprinkle with salt and pepper.

Add the water. Cover and cook on low for 5 to 6 hours, until the vegetables are very tender.

Transfer to a warmed serving dish and sprinkle with the parsley. Serve immediately.

TO DRINK Harp Lager or Newcastle Brown Ale, Britain's most popular bottled beer.

4 slices lean bacon

1 1/2 pounds pork sausages (6 to 8 sausages)

2 yellow onions, sliced

Salt and freshly ground black pepper

2 large potatoes, peeled and sliced

2 carrots, peeled and sliced

1 cup water, hard cider, chicken stock (page 101), or beer

1/4 cup chopped fresh parsley, for garnish

OATMEAL SOUP

Serves 4 to 6

Oats grow well in places that are too cold or damp for wheat, and consequently have been dietary staples throughout the British Isles for centuries. Thin oatcakes, cooked over an open flame, have long been the "tortillas" of Ireland. After baking soda was introduced in the nineteenth century, oatmeal soda breads became possible as well. Oats have also been used to brew delicious beers, and here they form the basis of a creamy, rich, and warming soup—a testament to the fact that good, simple ingredients, well prepared, can be delicious.

Heat a sauté pan over medium heat and add the butter. When melted, add the onion and sauté, stirring frequently, for 10 minutes, or until lightly browned. Transfer to the slow cooker.

Heat a dry small sauté pan over medium heat and add the oats and oat bran. Toast, stirring occasionally, for about 5 minutes, until lightly browned. Transfer to the slow cooker with the onion.

Add the stock to the slow cooker. Cover and cook on low for 6 to 8 hours, until the oats are very tender. Add the cream and salt and pepper to taste. Cover and cook for another 15 minutes to heat thoroughly.

Transfer to bowls and garnish with the parsley. Serve immediately.

TO DRINK Rhyne Cyder, a beautiful, delicate hard cider made in Sonoma County, California, or Newcastle Ale.

2 tablespoons unsalted butter

1 yellow onion, thinly sliced

1/3 cup steel-cut oats

1 tablespoon oat bran

3 cups chicken stock (page 101)

1 cup light cream or half-and-half

Salt and freshly ground black pepper

1/2 cup minced fresh parsley, for garnish

IRISH CHAMP

Serves 4 to 6

Potatoes, introduced to Ireland in the sixteenth century, soon became the mainstay of Ireland's rural poor. Champ—hand-mashed potatoes with any number of embellishments—was and is a favored dish.

Use the best ingredients you can find. Fresh organic potatoes, good salt, and high-quality butter will make this dish even more tasty. Traditionally, the scallions are simmered in milk before being added to the potatoes, but I prefer the texture of raw scallions. Chopped fresh parsley or chives, or fresh green peas, may be used instead of or in addition to the scallions.

Place the potatoes in the slow cooker and add the stock. Cover and cook on high for about 2 hours, until the potatoes are tender.

Transfer the potatoes to a bowl and mash with a potato masher. While the potatoes are still hot, add the milk, scallions, and 4 tablespoons of the butter. Mix well and season to taste with salt and pepper

Place the remaining 2 tablespoons butter on top of the potatoes to melt, and serve immediately.

TO DRINK Harp Lager or a good Irish tea.

6 large russet potatoes, peeled if desired and cut into chunks

1 cup chicken stock (page 101)

1 cup whole milk or half-and-half

1 bunch scallions, white and green parts, finely chopped

6 tablespoons unsalted butter

Salt and freshly ground black pepper

France

France is a country of varied climates and traditions. There are clear-cut distinctions among its regions, physically, culturally, and linguistically. To try and discuss "French cooking" in one breath is like trying to describe all the colors of the rainbow with one or two words.

Areas bordering the seas, rivers, and oceans have a plethora of fish dishes, while the cold climates in the eastern Jura Mountains and the Alps have more typical mountain food. The lands to the southeast are Mediterranean, both in approach to life and in choices of ingredients and cooking techniques.

If there is any one unifying factor among the cooking of France's many regions, perhaps it is the culinary use of local wines. All but one of the recipes in this chapter contain wine, usually specified only as "white" or "red" wine, though in France, the cook would naturally use the wine of the region.

France has many varieties of traditional earthenware casseroles for the preparation of one-pot meals, from *marmites* to gratin dishes. These dishes were often cooked all day in communal ovens, making them easily adapted to the slow cooker.

French Food and Drink

France is the mother of all wine-producing countries, and as such has been the gold standard for wine production for many years. Although there are a number of primary wine regions throughout the country (the Loire Valley, Alsace, Burgundy, the Rhône, and Bordeaux), there are also many secondary regions gaining in recognition and popularity. But make no mistake: wine is produced

BEEF BURGUNDY | PROVENÇAL BEEF STEW

CHICKEN PIPÉRADE | PROVENÇAL CHICKEN STEW

TARRAGON CHICKEN | PORK *with* PRUNES

FRENCH SPLIT PEA SOUP

everywhere in France, though it may be from a garden vineyard, or only for family consumption, or it may be for sale only to locals or for use in restaurants. So while there are many good books devoted to the subject of French wine, and many good French wines to be had here in the States, the best way to experience French wines is to travel through the French countryside with an open mind and a curious palate, tasting and eating as you go.

On my last trip to France, I spent some time in northern Provence and discovered some worthwhile wines in the Côteau du Tricastin, a small, southern Rhône appellation little known outside that country. In addition, I discovered the delicate Clairette de Die, a sparkling wine available only within a limited radius of the village of Die, and appreciated mostly as an aperitif.

Look to the wines of the region for good food pairings. Beef Burgundy, for instance, is traditionally made with Burgundy wine, so the most obvious beverage pairing would be a Burgundian wine. Certainly there is room for experimentation, but for regional foods, you can't go much wrong by pairing them with the traditional wines of their region.

BEEF BURGUNDY

Serves 4 to 6

Boeuf bourguignon is a quintessential Burgundian one-pot meal, combining the wine of the region with beef and herbs. Serve it over fresh noodles or with parsleyed potatoes.

Combine the flour and salt in a resealable plastic bag. Add the meat to the bag, several pieces at a time, and shake to coat completely.

Heat a large sauté pan over medium-high heat and add 2 tablespoons of the oil. In batches if necessary, add the beef and cook, turning, for 8 to 10 minutes, until browned on all sides. Using tongs, transfer to paper towels to drain, then arrange in the slow cooker.

Add the wine to the pan and stir over medium-high heat to scrape up the browned bits from the bottom of the pan. Cook, stirring frequently, for about 10 minutes, until the sauce begins to thicken. Stir in salt to taste. Add the garlic, thyme sprigs, and bay leaves. Pour over the beef in the slow cooker. Cover and cook on low for 6 to 8 hours, until the meat is very tender.

While the stew is cooking, peel and trim the onions. Heat a sauté pan over medium-high heat and add the remaining 1 tablespoon oil. Add the onions and sauté, stirring frequently, for 10 minutes, or until lightly browned. One hour before serving, add the onions to the stew and continue cooking until the onions are tender.

Heat a sauté pan over medium-high heat and add the butter. Add the mushrooms and sauté for 5 minutes, or until lightly browned. Add the mushrooms to the stew 30 minutes before serving. Remove the thyme sprigs and bay leaves. Transfer the stew to a soup tureen. Garnish with the chopped thyme and serve immediately.

TO DRINK Try a good medium-bodied Beaujolais.

$^3/_4$ cup all-purpose flour

1 teaspoon salt

$2^1/_2$ pounds beef stew meat, trimmed of fat, cut into $1^1/_2$-inch cubes

3 tablespoons vegetable or grapeseed oil

2 cups full-bodied red wine, such as Pinot Noir or Beaujolais

2 cloves garlic

2 sprigs thyme

2 bay leaves

20 baby white onions

1 tablespoon unsalted butter

1 pound button mushrooms, halved

$^1/_2$ cup chopped fresh thyme, for garnish

Provençal Beef Stew

Serves 4 to 6

This flavorful one-pot meal from the south of France could be made with either free-range veal or beef. The use of thyme, olives, garlic, olive oil, and particularly rosemary makes this dish truly representative of Provence.

Combine the flour and salt in a resealable plastic bag. Add the meat to the bag, several pieces at a time, and shake to coat completely.

Heat a large sauté pan over medium-high heat and add the oil. In batches if necessary, add the meat and cook, turning, for 7 to 10 minutes, until browned on all sides. Using tongs, transfer the meat to the slow cooker and add the thyme and rosemary.

Place the onions in the plastic bag and shake in the remaining flour to coat completely. Set the sauté pan over medium-high heat and add the onions. Sauté, stirring frequently, for about 10 minutes, until lightly browned. Add the garlic and sauté for 3 to 4 minutes, until softened. Add the wine to the pan and stir to scrape up the browned bits from the bottom of the pan. Add the tomatoes and whisk in the mustard and pepper to taste. Cook, stirring frequently, for 10 minutes, or until the sauce thickens somewhat. Pour the sauce over the meat in the slow cooker.

Cover and cook on low for 5 to 8 hours, until the meat is very tender. Stir in the olives 20 minutes before the end of cooking. Remove and discard the thyme and rosemary.

Ladle into soup bowls and serve immediately.

TO DRINK A Côtes de Provence rosé or a medium-bodied red table wine would do well here.

$^3/_4$ cup all-purpose flour

1 teaspoon salt

$2^1/_2$ pounds beef stew meat, cut into $1^1/_2$-inch cubes

2 to 3 tablespoons olive oil

2 sprigs thyme

2 sprigs rosemary

2 yellow onions, sliced

4 cloves garlic, minced

1 cup dry white wine

1 ($14^1/_2$-ounce) can crushed tomatoes

2 tablespoons Dijon mustard

Freshly ground black pepper

$1^1/_2$ cups green olives, pitted

CHICKEN PIPÉRADE

Serves 4 to 6

This recipe is adapted from one given me by my friend Pascal Vignau, the talented executive chef at the Four Seasons Aviara in Carlsbad, California. Pascal was born and raised in a small village in southwestern France. This recipe is from his neck of the woods. The word pipérade *refers to the sliced bell peppers in the recipe. Pascal says rabbit is often substituted for chicken in France.*

Combine the flour and salt in a resealable plastic bag. Add the chicken to the bag, several pieces at a time, and shake to coat completely.

Heat a large sauté pan over medium-high heat. Add the bacon and cook, turning, for 5 to 8 minutes, until crisp. Using tongs, transfer to paper towels to drain.

Wipe most of the bacon fat out of the pan, leaving a coating on the bottom. Add the chicken to the pan over medium-high heat and cook, turning once, for 10 minutes, until browned on both sides. Using tongs, transfer to paper towels to drain, then arrange in the slow cooker.

Set the sauté pan over medium-high heat and add the onion. Sauté, stirring frequently, for 10 to 15 minutes, until browned. Add the bell peppers and garlic and cook for 3 to 4 minutes, until softened. Add the tomatoes, tomato paste, wine, and pepper to taste and cook, stirring frequently, for 10 to 15 minutes, until the mixture begins to thicken.

Crumble the bacon over the chicken in the slow cooker and pour in the sauce. Add the thyme and bay leaves. Cover and cook on low for 3 to 8 hours, until the chicken is tender. At 3 to 4 hours, the chicken will still be firm and hold its shape. At 6 to 8 hours, the meat will be falling off the bone. Remove and discard the thyme and bay leaves.

Divide the chicken and sauce among plates and serve immediately.

TO DRINK A tannic, full-bodied red wine.

$^3/_4$ cup all-purpose flour

1 teaspoon salt

1 chicken, cut into serving pieces and skinned

3 to 4 strips bacon

1 yellow onion, sliced

3 red bell peppers, cut into strips

6 cloves garlic, crushed

1 (14$^1/_2$-ounce) can crushed or chopped tomatoes

2 tablespoons tomato paste

1 cup dry white wine

Freshly ground black pepper

1 sprig thyme

2 bay leaves

Provençal Chicken Stew

Serves 4 to 6

This simple chicken stew draws on the characteristic flavors of Provence: tomatoes, basil, olives, olive oil, and garlic. This dish was traditionally made in an earthenware casserole such as those produced in the Provençal town of Vallauris, located in the Alpes-Maritimes above Cannes. Vallauris has been home to producers of such casseroles for centuries and has been a pottery center in France since the nineteenth century.

Combine the ¾ cup flour and the salt in a resealable plastic bag. Add the chicken to the bag, several pieces at a time, and shake to coat completely.

Heat a large sauté pan over medium-high heat and add the oil. Add the chicken and cook, turning once, for 8 to 10 minutes, until browned on both sides. Using tongs, transfer to paper towels to drain, then arrange in the slow cooker.

Set the sauté pan over medium-high heat and add the onion and the 2 tablespoons flour. Sauté, stirring frequently, for 10 minutes, or until lightly browned. Add the garlic and stir for 2 to 3 minutes. Add the wine and stir to scrape up the browned bits from the bottom of the pan. Increase the heat to high and add the tomatoes and pepper to taste. Cook, stirring frequently, for 10 to 15 minutes, until some of the tomato liquid evaporates.

Pour the onion mixture over the chicken in the slow cooker. Cover and cook on low for 3 to 8 hours, until the chicken is tender. At 3 to 4 hours, the chicken will still be firm and hold its shape. At 6 to 8 hours, the meat will be falling off the bone.

Divide the chicken among dinner plates and garnish with the parsley, basil, and olives. Serve immediately.

TO DRINK A dry, aromatic, and flavorful rosé.

3/4 cup plus 2 tablespoons all-purpose flour

1 teaspoon salt

1 chicken, cut into serving pieces and skinned

1/4 cup olive oil

1 yellow onion, finely chopped

1 clove garlic, minced

1/2 cup dry white wine

1 (14 1/2-ounce) can crushed tomatoes

Freshly ground black pepper

1/4 cup chopped fresh parsley, for garnish

1/4 cup fresh basil leaves, cut into chiffonade, for garnish

1 cup black Nyons or kalamata olives, for garnish

Tarragon Chicken

Serves 4 to 6

The first time I tasted this classic French dish was in a small café on a winding street in Montmartre, my favorite section of Paris. At the time, I thought it was one of the best things I had ever tasted. After adapting it to the slow cooker, I still think so today, some twenty years later.

Combine the ¾ cup flour and the salt in a resealable plastic bag. Add the chicken to the bag, several pieces at a time, and shake to coat completely.

Heat a sauté pan over medium-high heat and add the butter and oil. Add the chicken and cook, turning once, for 8 to 10 minutes, until browned on both sides. Using tongs, transfer to paper towels to drain, then arrange in the slow cooker.

Set the sauté pan over medium-high heat and add the onion and the 2 tablespoons flour. Sauté, stirring frequently, for 10 minutes, or until lightly browned. Gradually add the wine, stirring to scrape up the browned bits from the bottom of the pan. Add the stock and cook, stirring frequently, for 10 to 15 minutes, until the sauce is thick enough to coat the back of a spoon. Pour the sauce over the chicken in the slow cooker and lay 2 sprigs of the tarragon on top.

³/₄ cup plus 2 tablespoons all-purpose flour

1 teaspoon salt

1 chicken, cut into serving pieces and skinned

2 tablespoons unsalted butter

2 tablespoons olive oil

1 yellow onion, finely chopped

1 cup dry white wine

1 cup chicken stock (page 101)

6 sprigs tarragon

1 cup heavy cream or half-and-half

Cover and cook on low for 3 to 8 hours, until the chicken is tender. At 3 to 4 hours, the chicken will still be firm and hold its shape. At 6 to 8 hours, the meat will be falling off the bone. Pour in the cream and stir well. Cover and cook for 10 to 15 minutes to heat thoroughly.

While the chicken finishes cooking, strip the leaves from the remaining 4 sprigs of tarragon and chop coarsely. Remove and discard the tarragon sprigs from the slow cooker and stir in the freshly chopped tarragon.

Divide the chicken and sauce among plates and serve immediately.

TO DRINK A crisp, acidic Sauvignon Blanc such as Didier Dageneau's En Chailloux, or a good Sancerre or Pouilly-Fuissé.

PORK *with* PRUNES

Serves 4 to 6

Several areas in France are famous for prunes, including Agen in the Touraine. And although the combination of meat and fruit is not often found in France, roast pork with prunes is a traditional dish of Agen. The rich, soulful flavors of this slow cooker version make this dish one of my favorites.

Combine the ¾ cup flour and salt in a resealable plastic bag. Add the meat to the bag, several pieces at a time, and shake to coat completely.

Heat a large sauté pan over medium-high heat and add the oil. In batches if necessary, add the meat and cook, turning, for about 10 minutes, until browned on all sides. Using tongs, transfer the meat to the slow cooker.

Set the sauté pan over medium-high heat and add the onions and the 3 tablespoons flour. Sauté, stirring frequently, for 10 to 15 minutes, until browned. Gradually add the cider, stirring to scrape up the browned bits from the bottom of the pan. Add the stock and cook, stirring frequently, for 10 to 15 minutes, until the sauce thickens enough to coat the back of a spoon. Pour the sauce over the pork in the slow cooker and add the thyme, bay leaves, and prunes.

Cover and cook on low for 6 to 8 hours, until the sauce is thick and the meat is very tender. Remove and discard the thyme and bay leaves.

Transfer the meat to a cutting board and cut into serving portions. Divide among dinner plates and pour the sauce and prunes over each serving. Serve immediately.

TO DRINK I'm sure there is a wine out there that would complement this dish well, but for a combination you can't beat, try Belgian Gulden Draak (Golden Dragon) Ale, or another rich, fruity ale.

³⁄₄ cup plus 3 tablespoons all-purpose flour

1 teaspoon salt

2 pounds country-style spareribs or pork loin roast

1 tablespoon vegetable oil

2 yellow onions, thinly sliced

1 cup hard cider or white wine

1 cup chicken stock (page 101)

1 sprig thyme

2 bay leaves

1¹⁄₄ cups pitted prunes (8 ounces)

FRENCH SPLIT PEA SOUP

Serves 4 to 6

Potage Saint-Germain is a classic French soup. Created in the Île-de-France, its ingredients are both inexpensive and nourishing. It has been a workingman's favorite for years.

Note: This recipe was tested in a 3½-quart slow cooker (but could be made in any size cooker).

Rinse and sort through the split peas. Place the peas in the slow cooker and add the water, onion, carrots, celery, and pork chop.

Cover and cook on low for 8 to 10 hours, until the peas are tender and the meat has fallen away from the bone. Season with salt to taste. Remove and discard the pork chop bone and break up any large chunks of meat with a fork.

Ladle into bowls, dividing the meat evenly, and serve immediately.

TO DRINK I think beer would be a better choice here than wine; perhaps a Belgian beer such as that brewed by the Trappist monks at the Abbey of Chimay, or Duvel Belgian Ale, or any dark, fruity beer or ale.

2 cups split peas

6 cups water or chicken stock (page 101)

½ yellow onion, finely chopped

2 carrots, peeled and finely chopped

2 celery stalks, finely chopped

1 smoked pork chop

Salt

Italy

Traditions of earthenware cookery abound in Italy, and early samples of Italian pottery are found in the museums of each region. The evolution of slow-simmered one-pot meals in Italy is similar to that in agricultural regions around the Western world. The farm wife would put a cauldron or stew pot on the hearth in the morning, let it cook all day, and the meal would be ready when family members came home from an arduous day in the fields.

It is difficult to think of Italian cooking without also thinking of olives, olive oil, wine, and tomatoes. Olives, their oil, and wine have been with the Italian people for ages, but tomatoes, so much a part of their cuisines today, arrived only in the sixteenth century, and at first were considered fit only for the ornamental garden.

Although many Italians shop in the supermarkets today, older rural housewives tend to keep the traditions of slow cooking alive using ingredients from the countryside. As in Greece, it is still common to forage for wild greens in the spring for salads, soups, and stews; to pick and cure olives in the fall and winter; to hunt mushrooms in the winter and spring; and to pick tomatoes in the summer, sometimes drying them in the sun for use throughout the year.

In Italy, as in so many other countries, slow-cooked dishes are usually based on meat or beans, with one of the main differences being that beef may be found more regularly in Italy than elsewhere. And as in most other

POLENTA | SAUSAGE *and* SUN-DRIED TOMATO SAUCE

ITALIAN POT ROAST | TUSCAN WHITE BEAN SOUP

WHITE TRUFFLE RISOTTO | ARTICHOKE RISOTTO

NEAPOLITAN LAMB STEW | CHICKEN CACCIATORE

BREAD PUDDING | ANISE BISCOTTI

Mediterranean cultures, no self-respecting Italian would think a meal or much less a life complete without a well-made local wine in the pot or on the table.

Italian Food and Drink

Italian wines are the consummate food wines; for centuries, Italian wines have been made to accompany the foods of their own particular regions. With more than a thousand documented different grape varieties, the diversity is amazing. Only the more well-known Italian wines and grape varieties seem to make it outside of the country, so traveling in Italy can be an endless journey of discovery. (I always make it a point to leave as much room as possible in my suitcase when I go, so that I can cram interesting wines into every remaining nook and cranny for the trip home.)

Most of the Italian wines we Americans are familiar with come from the northern part of Italy, such as Barolo, Barbaresco, Chianti, Brunello, Dolcetto, and even Asti Spumante. Although more wines from other parts of the country are being imported to the United States, such as Primitivo from Puglia, northern Italian wines are the ones most likely to be available here. When choosing wines for Italian foods, a good rule of thumb is to look to the region—regional foods naturally pair with local wines.

POLENTA

Serves 4

In most parts of Europe, corn, a product of the Americas, is considered fit only for cattle. But there are a few places where corn or corn flour has won mainstream acceptance. The Portuguese, for instance, make a partly cornmeal bread called broa. *And the northern Italians go for polenta, coarsely ground dried corn, in a big way. Soft polenta is often served mounded on a plate with a sauce poured over the top. Although traditionally polenta requires fairly constant stirring, you can make an acceptable version in the slow cooker with very little effort.*

Polenta may be served in its creamy, just-cooked state or may be allowed to solidify, after which it can be sliced and sautéed, grilled, or fried prior to serving. Polenta can also take center stage in various rustic dishes where layers of it alternate with any number of other ingredients, usually ground meat or cheeses and some kind of sauce.

Combine all the ingredients in the slow cooker. Cover and cook on high for about 1½ hours, until the polenta is creamy and the grains are tender. Stir once or twice during cooking. Transfer to a serving dish and serve warm.

3 cups chicken stock (page 101) or water

1 teaspoon salt

1 cup polenta

TO DRINK Pair with whatever you're drinking with the main course.

Sausage *and* Sun-Dried Tomato Sauce

Serves 4 to 6

Although tomatoes are latecomers to Italian cuisine, slow-cooking tomato-based sauces have become the heart and soul of Italian cooking. Serve this sauce over pasta or a mound of creamy polenta.

In a small bowl, combine the sun-dried tomatoes and wine. Let soak for at least 30 minutes, until softened.

Combine the fennel and allspice in a mortar or coffee grinder and grind to a fine powder.

Heat a large sauté pan over medium-high heat and add the oil. Add the onion and sauté, stirring frequently, for 10 to 15 minutes, until browned. Add the garlic, celery, and carrots and sauté for 3 to 4 minutes, until lightly browned. Add the sausages and spice mixture and stir for 2 minutes, until well blended. Add the crushed tomatoes. Drain the sun-dried tomatoes, reserving the wine, and cut them into thin slices. Add the wine, sun-dried tomatoes, and salt and pepper to taste to the sauce and stir well.

Pour into the slow cooker and add the thyme. Cover and cook on low for 6 to 8 hours, until the flavors are well blended and the sauce is the thickness you prefer. Remove and discard the thyme before serving.

TO DRINK Try a hefty, complex Brunello from pioneer producer Biondi-Santi in Montalcino.

1 cup dry-packed sun-dried tomatoes (3 ounces)

1 cup hearty dry red wine

1 teaspoon fennel seed

3 allspice berries

2 tablespoons olive oil

1 large yellow onion, finely chopped

3 cloves garlic, minced

2 celery stalks, finely chopped

2 carrots, peeled and finely chopped

$1/2$ pound spicy Italian sausages, sliced

2 (28-ounce) cans crushed tomatoes

Salt and freshly ground black pepper

1 sprig thyme

ITALIAN POT ROAST

Serves 4 to 6

Pot roast is a big favorite throughout northern Italy, just as it is in the United States: a cut of beef stewed in a hearty red wine and tomato sauce. The longer you cook it, the better it gets, as the meat begins to fall away from the bone and meld into the sauce. It's delicious served over polenta. This dish is traditionally cooked in an earthenware casserole, glazed on the inside.

Combine the cinnamon, cloves, allspice, and peppercorns in a mortar or coffee grinder and grind to a fine powder.

Heat a large sauté pan over medium-high heat and add the oil. Add the meat and cook, turning, for 10 to 15 minutes, until browned on all sides. Using tongs, transfer to the slow cooker.

Add the onion to the sauté pan and sauté, stirring frequently, for 10 minutes, or until lightly browned. Add the garlic, celery, and carrots and sauté for 3 to 4 minutes, until lightly browned. Add the spice mixture and cook for 2 minutes. Add the red wine and cook for about 10 minutes, until reduced by about one-third. Stir in the crushed tomatoes and salt to taste. Pour the sauce over the meat in the slow cooker.

Cover and cook on low for about 8 hours, until the meat falls away from the bone.

Transfer to a warmed serving dish and garnish with the parsley. Serve immediately.

TO DRINK A full-bodied Barbera from the Piedmont region, from Pio Cesare or Renato Ratti. A domestic Barbera would also work, such as one from Louis Martini.

1 cinnamon stick, broken into pieces

4 whole cloves

3 allspice berries

6 black peppercorns

3 tablespoons olive oil

$3^1/_2$ pounds beef pot roast, trimmed of excess fat

1 yellow onion, finely chopped

4 cloves garlic, minced

2 celery stalks, sliced

2 carrots, peeled and sliced

1 cup hearty dry red wine

1 (28-ounce) can crushed tomatoes

Salt

Chopped fresh parsley, for garnish

Tuscan White Bean Soup

Serves 4 to 6

Here is Tuscany's version of the globally ubiquitous bean soup: simple white beans, laced with good olive oil and dusted with freshly grated Parmesan cheese.

Rinse and sort through the beans. Place them in the slow cooker and add enough of the water to cover. Cover and cook on high for 2 hours, or until the beans are somewhat tender. Or, soak the beans overnight in water to cover, then drain, rinse, and transfer to the slow cooker. Add the water to cover.

Add the carrot, onion, celery, garlic, thyme, and tomatoes and stir well. Cover and cook on low for 6 to 8 hours, until the carrot and beans are very tender. Stir in salt to taste. Remove and discard the thyme.

Ladle into soup bowls. Garnish each serving with 1 tablespoon olive oil and a sprinkle of cheese. Serve immediately.

TO DRINK A not-too-tannic or concentrated Chianti, such as Antinori Pèppoli. It's 90 percent Sangiovese and 10 percent Merlot: a clean, fragrant, fruity wine.

2 cups dried white beans, such as cannellini or navy

6 to 8 cups water

1 carrot, peeled and finely chopped

1 yellow onion, finely chopped

1 celery stalk, finely chopped

3 cloves garlic, minced

1 sprig thyme

1 (14 1/2-ounce) can crushed tomatoes

Salt

4 to 6 tablespoons olive oil, for garnish

Freshly grated Parmigiano-Reggiano cheese, for garnish

WHITE TRUFFLE RISOTTO

Serves 4

Alessandro Serni is the chef at Vivace, the Four Seasons Aviara's signature restaurant in Carlsbad, California. Alex, born in Barcelona and raised near Milan, makes the best risotto I've tasted anywhere. One of my favorite treats is to visit Vivace with a good book or a good friend and enjoy a plate of Alex's risotto with a big glass of Amarone or Barolo.

Risotto, though traditionally made on top of the stove, is a natural for the slow cooker. It does not require the fairly constant attention and stirring that it does when made on the stove top, but can simply be consigned to the slow cooker and left on its own.

Heat a large sauté pan over medium heat and add the oil. Add the shallots and garlic and sauté for about 3 minutes, until light golden. Add the rice and stir for 1 minute, or until opaque. Add the wine and cook, stirring occasionally, for about 10 minutes, until the liquid is reduced by two-thirds.

Transfer the rice mixture to the slow cooker and add the thyme and stock. Cover and cook on high for about 2 hours, until the rice is firm but tender. Stir in the butter, truffle oil, cheese, and salt and pepper to taste just before serving. Remove and discard the thyme.

Transfer to a warmed serving dish and garnish with cheese and shaved truffle. Serve immediately.

TO DRINK Stefano Farina's Barolo, a deep, gutsy red wine made from the Nebbiolo grape variety from Italy's Piedmont region.

3 tablespoons olive oil

3 shallots, minced

3 cloves garlic, minced

2 cups Arborio rice

1 cup dry white wine

2 sprigs thyme

6 cups chicken stock (page 101)

$1/4$ cup unsalted butter

2 tablespoon white truffle oil

6 tablespoons freshly grated Parmigiano-Reggiano cheese, plus more for garnish

Salt and freshly ground black pepper

Shaved white truffle, for garnish (optional)

ARTICHOKE RISOTTO

Serves 4

Here is another of Alessandro Serni's simple yet irresistible risottos from the Four Seasons Aviara restaurant, Vivace. It is best made in the springtime with fresh artichokes. If you can find tiny ones, use them cut in half. If not, cook large artichokes, eat the leaves, remove the chokes, and slice the hearts for the risotto.

Heat a large sauté pan over medium-high heat and add the oil. Add the onion and garlic and sauté, stirring frequently, for about 10 minutes, until lightly browned. Add the rice and stir for 1 minute, or until opaque. Add the wine and cook for about 10 minutes, until the liquid is reduced by two-thirds.

Transfer the rice mixture to the slow cooker and add the stock and artichokes. Cover and cook on high for about 2 hours, until the rice is firm but tender. Stir in the butter, cheese, and salt and pepper to taste just before serving.

Transfer to a warmed serving dish and garnish with cheese. Serve immediately.

TO DRINK Franco Fiorina's Barbaresco is a very big red wine made from the Nebbiolo grape that comes from the Piedmont region.

3 tablespoons olive oil

1/2 yellow onion, finely chopped

3 cloves garlic, minced

2 cups Arborio rice

1 cup dry white wine

6 cups chicken stock (page 101)

4 cooked small artichokes, quartered, or 2 cooked large artichokes hearts, sliced

1/4 cup unsalted butter

6 tablespoons freshly grated Parmigiano-Reggiano cheese, plus more for garnish

Salt and freshly ground black pepper

Neapolitan Lamb Stew

Serves 4 to 6

In Italy, as well as in Greece, lamb signifies springtime. As such, it is traditionally served at Easter. Roasted or stewed, and combined with the most simple garden ingredients, it makes a savory dish with pasta or roasted potatoes.

Heat a large sauté pan over medium-high heat. Add the bacon and fry for 7 minutes, or until crisp. Using tongs, transfer to paper towels to drain. Chop the bacon coarsely.

Combine the flour and salt in a resealable plastic bag. Add the lamb to the bag, several pieces at a time, and shake to coat completely.

Heat a large sauté pan over medium-high heat and add the oil. In batches if necessary, add the lamb and cook, turning, for 7 to 10 minutes, until browned on all sides. Using tongs, transfer the lamb to the slow cooker.

Add the onion to the same pan and sauté, stirring frequently, for 10 minutes, or until lightly browned. Add the celery and garlic and sauté for 3 to 4 minutes, until softened. Add the wine to the sauté pan and stir to scrape up the browned bits from the bottom of the pan.

Add the onion mixture, bacon, tomatoes, and rosemary to the lamb in the slow cooker and mix well.

Cover and cook on low for 6 to 8 hours, until the meat is very tender. Season with salt and pepper to taste. Remove and discard the rosemary.

Transfer to a warmed serving dish and garnish with the basil just before serving.

TO DRINK An interesting choice from the south of Italy would be a Primitivo from Puglia; it is the same grape as our Zinfandel. A Mano Primitivo is readily available in the States, reasonably priced and quite enjoyable.

Ingredients

- 4 slices bacon or pancetta
- $3/4$ cup flour
- 1 teaspoon salt
- $2^{1}/_{2}$ pounds lamb stew meat, cut into $1^{1}/_{2}$-inch cubes
- 2 to 3 tablespoons olive oil
- 1 large onion, chopped
- 1 celery stalk, chopped
- 3 cloves garlic, minced
- 1 cup red wine
- 2 pounds tomatoes, coarsely chopped
- 2 sprigs rosemary
- Freshly ground black pepper
- Fresh basil leaves, cut into chiffonade, for garnish

CHICKEN CACCIATORE

Serves 4 to 6

Cacciatore translates as "hunter-style," and many versions of this dish exist. The preparation was developed as a simple way to cook game birds, or in this case chicken, after a hunt.

Combine the flour and salt in a resealable plastic bag. Add the chicken to the bag, several pieces at a time, and shake to coat completely.

Heat a large sauté pan over medium-high heat and add the oil. Add the chicken and cook, turning once, for 10 minutes, or until browned on both sides. Using tongs, transfer to the slow cooker.

Add the onion to the sauté pan and sauté, stirring frequently, for 10 minutes, or until lightly browned. Add the garlic and sauté for 2 minutes, or until light golden. Add the sun-dried tomatoes and wine and stir to scrape up the browned bits from the bottom of the pan. Pour over the chicken in the slow cooker.

Add the sage, rosemary, and pepper flakes to the slow cooker. Cover and cook on low for 3 to 8 hours, until the chicken is tender. At 3 to 4 hours, the chicken will still be firm and hold its shape. At 6 to 8 hours, the meat will be falling off the bone. Stir in salt and pepper to taste just before serving. Remove and discard the sage and rosemary.

Divide the chicken and sauce among dinner plates and serve at once.

TO DRINK A full-bodied red Barbera d'Asti, such as Brovici's Brea, or even a domestic Barbera.

$^3/_4$ cup all-purpose flour

1 teaspoon salt

1 chicken, cut into serving pieces and skinned

3 tablespoons olive oil

1 yellow onion, finely chopped

4 cloves garlic, minced

3 tablespoons coarsely chopped oil-packed sun-dried tomatoes

1 cup dry white wine

2 sprigs sage

2 sprigs rosemary

Pinch of crushed red pepper flakes

Freshly ground black pepper

BREAD PUDDING

Serves 6 to 8

Bread pudding is found wherever frugal home cooks don't want to waste stale bread. Eggs and fruit are enrichments added for special occasions. This is the best, most flavorful bread pudding I've tasted, and it's very easy to make.

Grease the slow cooker well with butter. In a mortar or coffee grinder, grind the cinnamon stick to a fine powder.

Combine the bread, cherries, apricots, and almonds in the slow cooker.

In a bowl, combine the eggs, milk, half-and-half, sugar, vanilla, cinnamon, and nutmeg. Whisk until smooth. Pour over the bread and fruit in the slow cooker.

Cover and cook on low for 3 hours, or until the pudding is firm and lightly browned. Place the lid slightly ajar for the last 20 minutes of cooking to facilitate browning.

Spoon into dessert bowls, and serve warm with a drizzle of half-and-half.

TO DRINK Practically every wine region in the world produces some form of sweet dessert wine. In Italy, it's called Vin Santo, and good ones can be found from Tuscany.

1 cinnamon stick, broken into pieces

8 cups stale bread cubes, preferably raisin bread

1 cup dried sweet cherries or cranberries

1 cup dried apricots, chopped

1 cup blanched almonds, chopped

4 eggs

2^1/$_2$ cups milk

2 cups half-and-half, plus more for serving

2^1/$_2$ cups granulated sugar

2 tablespoons pure vanilla extract

^{1}/$_4$ nutmeg pod, grated

ANISE BISCOTTI

Serves 6 to 8

Another surprise from the slow cooker. These are not true biscotti, since they are not cooked a second time after slicing to crisp them, but in flavor they are very similar to the traditional Italian cookies. The slices from the ends will be quite crispy, while those from the center will be more cake–like in texture. They can be toasted if desired.

Grease the slow cooker insert with butter or almond oil. Cut a piece of waxed paper to fit in the bottom, and grease the waxed paper.

In a large bowl, beat the butter, sugar, salt, eggs, and anise extract together until light and fluffy. In a separate bowl, combine the flour, baking powder, aniseed, and almonds. Stir to mix. Add to the wet ingredients and stir until blended.

Spread the dough evenly in the bottom of the slow cooker. Cover and cook on low for 3 hours. Place the lid slightly ajar and continue to cook for 1 hour, so that some of the moisture can evaporate. The biscotti are done when a toothpick inserted into the center comes out clean. Turn off the cooker, remove the lid, and allow to cool for 15 to 20 minutes.

Invert the insert over a wire rack to remove the biscotti. Allow to cool completely. On a cutting board, cut in half lengthwise, then cut each piece crosswise into 1-inch slices.

TO DRINK Biscotti are traditionally dipped in either Vin Santo or coffee.

$^1/_2$ cup unsalted butter, at room temperature, or $^1/_2$ cup almond oil

$1^1/_4$ cups sugar

$^1/_4$ teaspoon salt

3 eggs

$^1/_4$ teaspoon pure anise extract (optional)

$2^1/_2$ cups all-purpose flour

1 teaspoon baking powder

1 tablespoon aniseed

1 cup coarsely chopped blanched almonds

Greece

When most of us think of Greek food, we think of olives, pita bread, tomato-and-cucumber salads, and perhaps grilled fish or lamb, but the foods of Greece, like its people and terrain, vary widely from region to region. Mountain cooking from the north; clean, simple dishes from the Aegean Islands; and rich, spicy dishes from Asia Minor combine to make up Greek cuisine, as diverse as that of its better-known European neighbors.

The mountainous regions of Greece embrace the traditions of mountain dwellers everywhere: the people are often nomadic, and their cooking is dairy and meat based. Common themes are cheese dishes and long-cooked stews of goat or lamb so tender that, as one Greek friend put it, "you can cut it like butter." Olive trees don't grow well in the mountains, so olives, usually considered inseparable from Greek culture and cuisine, do not traditionally form an important element in the cooking of the these regions.

Moussaka, considered the quintessential Greek dish by many Americans, didn't arrive on the Greek scene until it was imported, along with many other spicy dishes, by the influx of immigrants from Asia Minor in the early years of the twentieth century. A spicy Venetian influence shows up in the cooking of the Ionian Islands, but the one unifying factor throughout the whole country is a use of whatever is at hand, whether animal or vegetable. What better way to do so than incorporating available ingredients into one pot, then simmering them for hours to develop depth, tenderness, and flavor?

The Greeks even have a name for this type of cooking: *yiahni* refers to one-pot meals containing beans, meat, and/or vegetables, spiked with plenty of onions and tomatoes. Such dishes have been

MOUSSAKA | LAMB SHANKS *in* TOMATO SAUCE

CHICKEN *with* LEMON-EGG SAUCE | BEAN SOUP

BAKED EGGPLANT | RICE PUDDING | WALNUT CAKE

cooked in unglazed earthenware casseroles since before Greece's golden age, and some unique types of clay pots have given their names to dishes, such as the conical-topped *kapama*.

Greek Food and Drink

Although its best-known wine is retsina (a white wine with added pine tree resin), Greece possesses a remarkable wealth of indigenous grape varieties that are used in the making of fine wines. In fact, Greece is one of the few countries that hasn't completely sold out to the production of Chardonnay, Cabernet, and a few other internationally popular grape varieties. Varieties with names like Roditis, Xinomavro, Assyrtiko, and Malagousia await the adventurous wine drinker. Most Greek wines tend to be dry and acidic, the perfect fit for a wide range of foods.

Finding Greek wines for sale in this country may be challenging. Sotiris Bafitis, a dedicated and passionate importer of fine Greek wines, is a wellspring of information about all things vinous and Greek. The two mail order sources for Greek wine listed at the end of this book work closely with Bafitis and can obtain any of the wines recommended in this chapter if they do not already have them in stock.

MOUSSAKA

Serves 4 to 6

You might say moussaka is to modern Greeks what mac'n'cheese is to most Americans. And although the version found in Greek–American restaurants is always made with ground beef or lamb, in Greece, vegetarian moussaka is common, especially during Lent. For a good vegetarian version of this dish, omit the meat and add sliced cooked artichoke hearts.

Traditionally, the eggplant slices are fried in olive oil before being consigned to the casserole, but skipping that step saves both time and calories.

Grease the slow cooker insert with olive oil.

Arrange the potato slices in a layer in the bottom of the slow cooker. Arrange the eggplant slices on top of the potato.

Combine the cinnamon, cloves, peppercorns, allspice, and cayenne in a mortar or coffee grinder and grind to a fine powder.

Heat a large sauté pan over medium-high heat. Add the meat, onion, and garlic and cook for about 8 minutes, until just browned. Break the meat into small clumps as it cooks. Add the spice mixture, wine, and tomatoes and simmer, stirring occasionally, for 10 minutes, or until the liquid is nearly all absorbed and the sauce has thickened. Stir in salt to taste. Spread the meat mixture on top of the potato and eggplant slices in the slow cooker. Cover and cook on low for 3 hours, until the potatoes are tender and the meat is cooked through.

To prepare the topping, combine the milk and flour in a saucepan and whisk until smooth. Place over medium-high heat and cook, stirring constantly, for 10 to 15 minutes, until thick enough to coat the back of a spoon. Add several pinches of nutmeg and stir well. Remove from the heat and beat in the eggs one at a time. Add the cheese and stir well.

1 large potato, peeled and thinly sliced

1 small eggplant, peeled and cut into $1/4$-inch-thick crosswise slices

1 cinnamon stick, broken into pieces

5 whole cloves

6 peppercorns

2 allspice berries

$1/4$ teaspoon cayenne pepper

1 pound very lean ground lamb or beef

1 large yellow onion, chopped

4 large cloves garlic, minced

$1/2$ cup dry red wine, preferably Greek

3 large tomatoes, peeled and diced, or 1 ($14^{1/2}$-ounce) can crushed tomatoes

Salt

Pour the topping over the meat in the slow cooker. Cover and cook on high for 2 hours, or until the topping is somewhat firm and slightly browned. Leave the lid slightly ajar for the last 30 minutes to encourage browning, if you like.

Turn off the slow cooker and let stand for about 30 minutes before serving. Spoon onto dinner plates and serve warm.

TO DRINK Malagousia is a unique aromatic white Greek grape variety that produces fairly full-bodied white wines. I recommend Gerovassiliou's Malagousia or a delicious, acidic Xinomavro rosé from Kir-Yianni winery called Akakies.

Topping

3 cups low-fat milk

$^1/_2$ cup all-purpose flour

Freshly grated nutmeg

2 eggs

1 cup shredded Gruyère cheese

LAMB SHANKS *in* TOMATO SAUCE

Serves 4

Lamb is unquestionably the most popular meat in Greece. Kapama *usually refers to any dish cooked in a tomato sauce flavored with cinnamon and cloves, but the word also refers to the traditional glazed earthenware casserole dish with a conical lid in which these stews are cooked. This dish goes well with noodles or roasted, grilled, or baked small potatoes, and a salad of spring greens.*

Lamb shanks, even when well trimmed, contain a lot of fat. If you prefer a leaner dish, make this one day ahead of time, refrigerate it, then remove the congealed fat. Or, buy a butterflied leg of lamb, trim it of all fat, and cut the meat into 1½-inch cubes.

Combine the cinnamon, cloves, and allspice in a mortar or coffee grinder and grind to a fine powder.

Heat a large sauté pan over medium-high heat and add the oil. Add the lamb and cook, turning, for 7 to 10 minutes, until browned on all sides. Using tongs, transfer the lamb to the slow cooker.

Add the onion to the sauté pan and cook, stirring frequently, for 10 minutes, or until lightly browned. Add the spice mixture and brandy to the onion and stir for 2 to 3 minutes to scrape up the browned bits from the bottom of the pan. Add the tomatoes and stir well. Pour over the lamb shanks in the slow cooker.

Cover and cook on low for 6 to 8 hours, until the meat is very tender and easily comes away from the bone. Season with salt and pepper to taste.

Divide the lamb and sauce among dinner plates and serve immediately.

TO DRINK Xinomavro is a grape variety indigenous to Macedonia in northern Greece that produces a fairly full-bodied, acidic red wine. Ktima Voyatzis's Red Table Wine is a stellar example of Xinomavro, blended with a bit of Cabernet and Merlot.

1 cinnamon stick, broken into pieces

4 whole cloves

8 allspice berries

1 tablespoon olive oil

4 lamb shanks, trimmed

1 large yellow onion, chopped

¼ cup Metaxa (Greek brandy) or other brandy

2 cups peeled and coarsely chopped fresh tomatoes, or 1 (14½-ounce) can crushed tomatoes

Salt and freshly ground black pepper

CHICKEN *with* LEMON-EGG SAUCE

Serves 4 to 6

In most agrarian cultures, meat was reserved for special occasions. Why kill the family hen when she was an on-going source of protein in the form of the egg? Kotopoulo avgolemono is a special dish combining both chicken and egg; the sauce is probably the best known of all Greek sauces. Though it is traditionally made with only egg, lemon, and stock, a bit of flour is added here for stability.

Place the mushrooms in a bowl and cover with warm water. Soak for 30 minutes, or until plumped. Drain and rinse thoroughly to remove any sand or dirt.

Combine the ¾ cup flour and the salt in a resealable plastic bag. Add the chicken to the bag, several pieces at a time, and shake to coat completely.

Heat a large sauté pan over medium-high heat and add the oil. Add the chicken and cook, turning, for 7 to 10 minutes, until browned on both sides. Using tongs, transfer to paper towels to drain.

Set the sauté pan over medium-high heat and add the onion and the 2 tablespoons flour. Sauté, stirring frequently, for 10 minutes, or until lightly browned. Gradually add the wine, stirring to scrape up the browned bits from the bottom of the pan. Add the stock and cook, stirring constantly, for 15 minutes, or until the sauce is thick enough to coat the back of a spoon. Add the mushrooms and stir well.

2 ounces dried wild mushrooms

¾ cup plus 2 tablespoons all-purpose flour

1 teaspoon salt

1 chicken, cut into serving pieces and skinned

3 tablespoons olive oil

1 yellow onion, thinly sliced

1 cup dry white wine

1 cup chicken stock (page 101)

4 cooked artichoke hearts, thickly sliced; 8 cooked baby artichokes, halved; 1 (8-ounce) box frozen artichokes, thawed; or 1 (14-ounce) can artichoke hearts

Layer the chicken and artichokes in the slow cooker. Pour the mushroom mixture and any pan juices over the chicken and artichokes. Cover and cook on low for 4 to 6 hours, until the chicken is tender. Arrange the chicken, artichokes, and mushrooms on a platter.

To the juices remaining in the slow cooker, add the lemon juice and egg yolks, and whisk until smooth and thickened. Pour the sauce over the chicken and vegetables on the platter and garnish with the parsley and oregano.

TO DRINK Try a bottle of "new wave" retsina from Gaia Wines. It is more lightly resinated and is a higher-quality wine than those commonly served in Greek taverns. Or, try a dry white wine made from the Roditis grape, such as Foloi, produced by Mercouri Estate.

$1/4$ cup freshly squeezed lemon juice

2 egg yolks

Chopped fresh parsley, for garnish

Leaves from 3 sprigs oregano, chopped, for garnish

Bean Soup

Serves 4 to 6

The Greeks have a saying: "Beans are life." Although bean soup is popular throughout Greece, it is especially so in the northern parts of the country, where the climate is cold and damp.

Rinse and sort through the beans. Place them in the slow cooker and add enough of the water to cover. Cover and cook on high for about 2 hours, until the beans begin to soften. Or, soak the beans with water to cover overnight, then drain, rinse, and transfer to the slow cooker. Add the water to cover.

Heat a large sauté pan over medium-high heat and add the oil. Add the onion, carrots, celery, and garlic and sauté, stirring frequently, for 10 minutes, or until lightly browned. Add the vegetables and ham bone to the beans in the slow cooker. Cover and cook on low for 6 to 8 hours, until the beans are tender. (At this point, you can purée some of the beans for a thicker consistency if you like.)

A few minutes before serving, stir in the tomatoes, oregano, spinach, and salt. Ladle the soup into bowls and garnish with the parsley. Serve immediately.

TO DRINK A light red wine like Oktana's Aghiorghitiko (a grape variety known in English as St. George), a Pinot Noir–style wine from Nemea. Or, choose any French or American Pinot Noir.

2 cups dried white beans

6 to 8 cups water or chicken stock (page 101)

2 tablespoons olive oil

1 yellow onion, finely chopped

3 carrots, peeled and finely diced

3 celery stalks, finely chopped

2 large cloves garlic, minced

1 ham bone (optional)

3 large ripe tomatoes, peeled and diced, or 1 ($14^1/2$-ounce) can crushed tomatoes

Leaves from 2 sprigs oregano, coarsely chopped

1 cup packed spinach leaves, young dandelion greens, or arugula

1 tablespoon salt

$^1/_4$ cup chopped fresh parsley, for garnish

BAKED EGGPLANT

Serves 4 to 6

Many Greek dishes are vegetarian, as rural people have always had to rely on what they could grow in their own gardens or obtain nearby. In addition, many Greeks observe the Lenten season by giving up all animal foods, so quite a few vegetarian options have been developed for that time of year. This very simple vegetarian dish can be served hot, over rice or pasta with an herb-and-feta garnish, or cold as a salad, scooped up with pita.

Note: This dish is an exception to the don't-fill-the-slow-cooker-more-than-two-thirds-full rule. Here, the cooker is filled to the top, as the eggplant compresses greatly as it cooks.

Pour ¼ cup of the olive oil into the slow cooker and rotate to coat the bottom. Add the eggplant and the remaining ¼ cup oil and toss lightly. Cover and cook on high for about 2 hours or on low for about 5 hours, until the eggplant is quite mushy. Stir two or three times during cooking.

Add the garlic, lemon juice, and salt to taste, and stir well to break up any large chunks of eggplant. Transfer to a bowl, drizzle with extra virgin olive oil, and garnish with the parsley, mint, and feta. Serve hot as a main course or cold as an appetizer.

TO DRINK Argyros Estate's Santorini 2000, a white of some substance made from the Assyrtiko grape, or Kir-Yianni's light, dry, acidic Xinomavro rosé, Akakies.

½ cup olive oil

3 eggplants, peeled and cut into cubes

3 cloves garlic, pressed

Juice of 1 lemon

Salt

Extra virgin olive oil, for drizzling (optional)

¼ cup chopped fresh parsley, for garnish

¼ cup coarsely chopped fresh mint leaves, for garnish

4 ounces fresh feta cheese, crumbled, for garnish (1 scant cup)

RICE PUDDING

Serves 4 to 6

Every Greek cookbook has a recipe for rizogalo, *so popular in Greece that it is sold in small cups on city streets. The formula is uniform and simple: rice, sugar, milk, cinnamon, vanilla, and sometimes lemon peel or zest. For a richer version, eggs may be added.*

Combine all the ingredients in the slow cooker and mix well. Cover and cook, stirring occasionally, on low for 4 hours, or until thick and creamy.

Transfer the pudding to individual dessert bowls or a large serving dish and refrigerate for 2 to 3 hours. Serve cold, or warm through before serving.

TO DRINK Follow this dessert with Greek coffee.

1 cup Arborio rice

5 cups whole milk

^{2}/3 cup sugar

1 tablespoon pure vanilla extract

^{1}/2 cinnamon stick, broken into pieces and finely ground

Pinch of salt

Walnut Cake

Serves 6 to 8

Walnuts are ubiquitous in Greek cuisine, as in much of Mediterranean cooking. Olive oil, rather than butter, would be the more traditional Greek cooking fat, and the fat-of-choice during the Lenten season.

Traditionally, this cake is baked in a sheet, then cut into diamond shapes, but baking it in the slow cooker works beautifully. The cake is excellent with tea, or toasted for breakfast. If tightly wrapped, it also freezes well. Serve it with or without the syrup poured over the top.

Grease the bottom and sides of the slow cooker insert with butter or oil. Cut a piece of waxed paper to fit in the bottom, then grease the waxed paper as well.

Combine the cinnamon, peppercorns, nutmeg, and cloves in a mortar or coffee grinder and grind to a fine powder.

In a food processor, combine the butter, sugar, yogurt, and eggs and process until smooth. Add the spice mixture, flour, baking powder, and baking soda and pulse until just blended. Stir in the walnuts by hand.

Pour the batter into the prepared slow cooker. Cover and bake on high for 2 hours, or until a toothpick inserted into the center of the cake comes out clean. Remove the insert from the cooker and allow the cake to cool for at least 30 minutes in the insert.

To prepare the syrup, combine all the ingredients in a small saucepan over medium-high heat and bring to a boil. Stir until the sugar dissolves. Decrease the heat to achieve a low boil and cook for about 10 minutes, until the syrup thickens. Remove from the heat and allow to cool. Remove and discard the lemon zest and cinnamon stick.

2 cinnamon sticks, broken into pieces

4 to 6 black peppercorns

$1/2$ teaspoon ground nutmeg

4 to 6 whole cloves

$1/2$ cup unsalted butter, at room temperature, or $1/2$ cup mild olive oil

2 cups sugar

1 cup nonfat plain yogurt

6 eggs

2 cups all-purpose flour

1 teaspoon baking powder

1 teaspoon baking soda

$1^{1}/2$ cups chopped walnuts

Drizzle the syrup over the cake and let stand until the syrup is completely absorbed. Remove the cake from the insert by running a knife around the edges of the cake. Place a wire rack on top of the insert, then invert the cake onto the rack. Allow to cool completely.

Cut the cake in half lengthwise, then cut each piece crosswise into slices. Place the slices on dessert plates and serve at once.

TO DRINK Montofoli Estate's Sweet White Dessert Wine produced from Assyrtiko, Athiri, Aidani, and Liatiko, all indigenous Greek grape varieties, or any dessert or late-harvest wine. Alternatively, a cup of strong black coffee would be a good accompaniment to this rich cake.

Simple Syrup

1^1/$_2$ cups sugar

1 thick strip lemon zest

1 cup water

1 cinnamon stick

India

India doesn't really have a strong tradition of slow-cooked oven-baked meals. For centuries, Indians have done their slow cooking, usually in the center of the kitchen, over an open fire. Wood fires gave way to coal, then gas stoves. Even today, as modern Indians adopt Western traditions and modern Indian kitchens take on the look of their Western counterparts, stove-top cooking takes precedence. The pressure cooker has become as common in the Indian repertoire as the frying pan.

The majority of Indians are vegetarian. Some are vegan, some include fish and dairy products in their diet (Indians from coastal areas often refer to fish as "fruits of the sea" and consider themselves vegetarian), and some include small amounts of meat from time to time.

You may be wondering about all those chicken, lamb, and beef curries found on the menus at Indian restaurants. Truth be told, most of what we in the Western world experience as "Indian cooking" is the cooking of northern India and, more specifically, of Punjab. (What is now Pakistan was at one time western Punjab.) After partition, refugees from that region poured into cities throughout India and around the world, opening restaurants based on the meat-rich cuisine of northern India.

The many northern Indian meat dishes and the legume and grain dishes from all over the country lend themselves well to long, slow cooking. This chapter includes one dish that has been traditionally cooked in an earthenware pot, sealed around the edges with dough to keep moisture and flavor within: the biryani. This rice dish comes into the Indian repertoire from the Muslims, or Moghuls, of the north. Other recipes in this chapter represent the adaptation of stove-top cuisine to the slow cooker.

EGGPLANT *and* PEA CURRY | CHICKEN CURRY

APRICOT CHICKEN | DAL | LAMB STEW *with* SPINACH

BEEF BIRYANI | CHICKEN *in* SAFFRON-TOMATO CREAM SAUCE

KEEMA-STUFFED PEPPERS

Indian Food and Drink

India is not a country with a lengthy history of wine production. Grape wines may have been produced there in the days of Alexander the Great, but the art was not sustained. There is a small and growing wine industry developing in India today, but it is, as yet, untested.

Some of the same suggestions that apply to choosing wines for Mexican foods also apply to choosing wines for Indian foods. Since tannins accentuate heat and spice, it is best to steer clear of bold, tannic red wines, and choose instead lighter, fruitier reds, like young Zinfandels or fruit-forward Syrahs. Gewürztraminers and Rieslings also pair well with spicy foods.

Aromatic Rhône whites, such as Viognier, Marsanne, and Roussane, work well. Or, try one of the medium-bodied white wines from Spain's Rueda district. Because the wines of Rueda are not well publicized, you can often pick them up at bargain prices. Greek wines like Assyrtiko or Malagousia fall into the same category, and would make perfect matches for certain Indian dishes.

Sparkling wines are also good companions to the spicy flavors of Indian cuisine. A blanc de blancs or a blanc de noirs would work well, or one of the more intensely flavored sparkling Shirazes coming out of Australia.

Fruity Belgian beers offer some interesting flavor and aroma to complement spicy Indian dishes as well, and Indian beer, long a favorite beverage in India, is always a good option.

EGGPLANT *and* PEA CURRY

Serves 4 to 6

The word curry *is not Indian, but an English invention. Some authorities believe it may have come from the Indian word* kari, *which means "sauce." Whatever the case, it is probably the word most commonly associated with Indian food in Western minds. Few Indian cooks own a jar of curry powder, however. Blending and grinding a unique spice mixture by hand is considered one of the hallmarks of a good Indian cook.*

As with most curries, this one is best served over rice. Do not let the apparently long list of ingredients in this and other Indian recipes discourage you. Most are spices, and once your larder is stocked, it is but the work of minutes to pull the appropriate spices out of the cupboard and grind them up.

Combine the coriander, cumin, and cinnamon in a mortar or coffee grinder and grind to a fine powder.

Heat a large sauté pan over medium-high heat and add the oil. Add the onions and sauté, stirring frequently, for 10 minutes, until lightly browned. Add the garlic and ginger and sauté for 30 seconds. Add the spice mixture, turmeric, paprika, and pepper flakes and stir for 2 minutes. Add the tomatoes and cook, stirring occasionally, for 10 minutes, or until some of the liquid evaporates.

Transfer the mixture to a blender and purée until almost smooth.

Place the eggplant in the bottom of the slow cooker and pour the puréed vegetables over the top. Stir gently.

Cover and cook on low for 3 to 4 hours, until the eggplant is tender. Stir in the peas during the last 15 minutes of cooking and season with salt to taste. Transfer to a serving dish and garnish with the cilantro.

TO DRINK A Greek Malagousia, a medium-bodied, aromatic white wine, or a Rhône white blend from California.

1 tablespoon coriander seed

1 tablespoon cumin seed

2 cinnamon sticks, broken into pieces

2 to 3 tablespoons vegetable oil

3 large yellow onions, finely chopped

2 large cloves garlic, minced

1 tablespoon grated or finely minced fresh ginger

1 teaspoon ground turmeric

1 tablespoon sweet paprika

1/2 teaspoon crushed red pepper flakes

2 large tomatoes, peeled and chopped, or 1 (14 1/2-ounce) can crushed tomatoes

2 large eggplants, peeled and cut into 1-inch cubes

1 cup fresh or frozen peas

Salt

1/4 cup coarsely chopped cilantro, for garnish

CHICKEN CURRY

Serves 4 to 6

My favorite Indian restaurant is Neela Paniz's Bombay Café at the intersection of Bundy and Pico in Los Angeles. Though the restaurant is small and unassuming, its food is imaginative, colorful, and fresh. This is my version of Neela's chicken curry, which, served with rice, is the dish probably most well-known by American lovers of Indian food.

Combine the cardamom, cinnamon, cloves, peppercorns, coriander, and cumin in a mortar or coffee grinder and grind to a fine powder.

Heat a large sauté pan over medium-high heat and add the oil. Add the onions and sauté, stirring frequently, for 10 to 15 minutes, until browned. Add the garlic, ginger, and chiles and stir for 1 to 2 minutes. Add the spice mixture, turmeric, cayenne, and salt and stir for 2 to 3 minutes. Stir in the tomatoes and cook for 5 to 6 minutes, until some of the liquid has evaporated.

Arrange the chicken in the slow cooker.

Transfer three-quarters of the onion mixture to a blender and purée until almost smooth. Pour the puréed vegetables and the reserved sautéed vegetables over the chicken in the slow cooker.

Cover and cook on low for 3 to 8 hours, until the chicken is tender. At 3 to 4 hours, the chicken will still be firm and hold its shape. At 6 to 8 hours, the meat will be falling off the bone. Transfer to a serving dish and garnish with the cilantro.

TO DRINK Chalk Hill Winery Pinot Gris. This rich, fruity product from Sonoma County's Chalk Hill appellation is a perfect match for this or just about any curry.

Seeds from 2 black cardamom pods

2 cinnamon sticks, broken into pieces

4 to 5 whole cloves

5 to 6 black peppercorns

1 tablespoon coriander seed

1 tablespoon cumin seed

1/4 cup vegetable oil

2 small yellow onions, finely chopped

5 to 6 cloves garlic, minced

1/2-inch piece fresh ginger, peeled and grated or minced

2 green serrano chiles, seeded and minced

1/4 teaspoon ground turmeric

1/4 teaspoon cayenne pepper

1 1/2 teaspoons salt

2 ripe tomatoes, coarsely chopped

1 chicken, cut into serving pieces and skinned

Chopped cilantro, for garnish

APRICOT CHICKEN

Serves 4 to 6

Apricots, like many of our favorite stone fruits, originated in the northern regions of India, Afghanistan, and Iran. This dish may well have come to India with the Parsis, a Zoroastrian sect from northern Persia (modern-day Iran) that settled in western India. Apricots have long been popular in Indian cooking, often in combination with meats. This particular combination is best served with rice and chapati. Chicken is always skinned in Indian dishes.

Combine the cinnamon and cardamom in a mortar or coffee grinder and grind to a fine powder.

Heat a large sauté pan over medium-high heat and add the oil. Add the onions and sauté, stirring frequently, for 10 to 15 minutes, until browned. Add the garlic and ginger and stir for 3 to 5 minutes. Add the spice mixture, tomatoes, water, and salt and stir for 5 minutes.

Place the chicken in the slow cooker and pour the onion mixture over the top. Cover and cook on low for 3 to 8 hours, until the chicken is tender. At 3 to 4 hours, the chicken will still be firm and hold its shape. At 6 to 8 hours, the meat will be falling off the bone. Stir in the apricots and saffron water 30 minutes before the end of cooking. Transfer to a serving dish and serve immediately.

TO DRINK This dish pairs well with a relatively inexpensive sparkling wine such as Gloria Ferrer Royal Cuvée from Sonoma County.

1 cinnamon stick, broken into pieces

Seeds from 2 black cardamom pods

3 tablespoons vegetable oil

2 yellow onions, finely chopped

1 large clove garlic, minced

2-inch piece fresh ginger, peeled and finely grated or minced

2 large tomatoes, diced, or 1 (14 1/2-ounce) can crushed tomatoes

1 cup water or chicken stock (page 101)

2 teaspoons salt

1 chicken, cut into serving pieces and skinned

2 cups dried apricots

1 pinch saffron threads, soaked in 2 tablespoons water

Dal

Serves 4 to 6

Dal is the name of the everyday lentil dishes that are as common in India as cornflakes are in America. Lentils can be red, black, green, yellow, or brown, and there as many recipes for dal as there are regions and families in India. Dal can be made thick like a stew, or thin like a soup, depending on individual preferences.

Rinse the lentils thoroughly and place them in the slow cooker.

Heat a sauté pan over medium-high heat and add the butter. Add the onion and sauté, stirring frequently, for 10 to 15 minutes, until browned. Add the garlic and ginger and stir for 1 to 2 minutes without browning the garlic. Transfer to the slow cooker and add the water.

Cover and cook on low for 3 to 8 hours, until the lentils are the consistency you prefer. At 3 to 4 hours, the lentils will retain some shape. At 6 to 8 hours, the dal will be more soup-like.

To prepare the cilantro cream, combine the yogurt and cilantro in a small bowl and mix well.

Ladle the lentils into bowls and garnish with a sprinkle of cilantro and chiles. Spoon a dollop of the cilantro cream on each and serve immediately.

TO DRINK Try a New Zealand Sauvignon Blanc such as the one from Cloudy Bay, or any zesty Sauvignon Blanc.

2 1/2 cups red or yellow lentils

1 tablespoon unsalted butter or vegetable oil

1/2 yellow onion, finely chopped

3 to 4 cloves garlic, minced

1-inch piece fresh ginger, peeled and grated or minced

4 cups water or chicken stock (page 101)

Cilantro-Yogurt Cream

1 cup plain yogurt

1 tablespoon chopped cilantro

Chopped cilantro, for garnish

2 serrano chiles, seeded and minced, for garnish

LAMB STEW *with* SPINACH

Serves 4 to 6

A classic Moghul dish, usually served with rice, that can also be made with beef. This dish is traditionally cooked in an earthenware casserole with the lid sealed tightly with dough.

Combine the coriander and cumin in a mortar or coffee grinder and grind to a fine powder.

Combine the flour and salt in a resealable plastic bag. Add the lamb to the bag, several pieces at a time, and shake to coat completely.

Heat a large sauté pan over medium-high heat and add the oil. In batches if necessary, add the lamb and cook, turning, for 7 to 10 minutes, until browned on all sides. Using tongs, transfer to paper towels to drain.

Set the sauté pan over medium-high heat and add the onions. Sauté, stirring frequently, for 10 to 15 minutes, until browned. Add the spice mixture, garlic, ginger, paprika, and cayenne and stir for 1 to 2 minutes. Add the tomatoes and cook for 5 minutes, or until some of the liquid has evaporated.

Place the lamb in the slow cooker and add the onion mixture and yogurt. Stir well. Cover and cook on low for 6 to 8 hours, until the meat is very tender. Just before serving, stir in the spinach and season with salt to taste.

Transfer to a warmed serving dish. Garnish with the cilantro and serve immediately.

TO DRINK A light, fruity Zinfandel.

3 tablespoons coriander seed

2 tablespoons cumin seed

$3/4$ cup all-purpose flour

1 teaspoon salt

2 pounds lamb stew meat, trimmed of fat and cut into $1^1/2$-inch cubes

$1/4$ cup vegetable oil

2 yellow onions, finely chopped

2 cloves garlic, minced

1 tablespoon minced fresh ginger

1 tablespoon sweet paprika

$1/2$ teaspoon cayenne pepper

1 (28-ounce) can crushed tomatoes

$1/2$ cup plain yogurt

1 cup packed spinach leaves

Salt

$1/2$ cup packed cilantro leaves, chopped, for garnish

Beef Biryani

Serves 4 to 6

A traditional biryani is a festive one-pot meal of Moghul origins. Marinated meat, spices, and partially cooked basmati rice are laced with clarified butter and cooked in a tightly closed casserole until the meat is tender and the flavors are blended. Here, the rice is cooked separately and added at the end of the cooking time in order to preserve its texture. I have omitted the use of copious amounts of clarified butter.

Combine the cumin, cardamom, cloves, peppercorns, and cinnamon in a mortar or coffee grinder and grind to a fine powder.

Heat a large sauté pan over medium-high heat and add the oil. Add the beef and cook, turning, for 10 minutes, until browned on all sides. Using tongs, transfer to a plate.

Add the onion to the sauté pan and sauté, stirring frequently, for 10 to 15 minutes, until browned. Add the garlic and ginger and stir for 3 minutes. Add the spice mixture and stir well. Add the meat and yogurt and toss well.

Transfer to the slow cooker and stir in the water. Cover and cook on low for 6 to 8 hours, until the meat is very tender. Stir in the rice, peas, saffron water, and salt 30 minutes before the end of cooking.

Transfer to a serving dish and garnish with cilantro.

TO DRINK A medium-bodied Pinot Noir from either Santa Barbara County's Sanford Winery or the Carneros district of Sonoma County.

1 tablespoon cumin seeds

Seeds from 3 black cardamom pods

6 whole cloves

6 to 8 peppercorns

2 cinnamon sticks, broken into pieces

3 tablespoons vegetable oil

2 1/2 pounds beef sirloin, cut into 1 1/2-inch cubes

1 yellow onion, finely chopped

2 cloves garlic, minced

1-inch piece fresh ginger, peeled and grated or minced

1 cup plain yogurt

1 cup water

3 to 4 cups cooked rice, preferably basmati

1 cup fresh or frozen peas

1/2 teaspoon saffron threads, soaked in 1/4 cup water for 20 minutes

1 teaspoon salt

Chopped cilantro, for garnish

CHICKEN *in* SAFFRON-TOMATO CREAM SAUCE

Serves 4 to 6

Ghee (clarified butter) and yogurt are dietary staples for most Indians, but milk and cream appear much less often, making this dish somewhat unusual. It comes from the southwestern coast of the country, and should be served over rice.

Combine the cinnamon, cloves, coriander, and cumin in a mortar or coffee grinder and grind to a fine powder.

Heat a large sauté pan over medium-high heat and add the oil. Add the onions and sauté, stirring frequently, for 10 to 15 minutes, until browned. Add the spice mixture, garlic, ginger, chile, and salt and stir for 3 to 4 minutes. Stir in the tomatoes and cook for 5 minutes, or until some of the liquid has evaporated.

Place the chicken in the slow cooker and pour the onion mixture over the top. Cover and cook on low for 3 to 8 hours, until the chicken is tender. At 3 to 4 hours, the chicken will still be firm and hold its shape. At 6 to 8 hours, the meat will be falling off the bone.

In a small bowl, combine the saffron and half-and-half. Let soak for 30 minutes. Stir the saffron cream into the chicken 30 minutes before the end of cooking. Season with salt to taste. Transfer to a serving dish and garnish with the cilantro.

TO DRINK A medium-bodied Viognier from California.

1 cinnamon stick, broken into pieces

6 whole cloves

1 tablespoon coriander seed

1 tablespoon cumin seed

3 tablespoons vegetable oil

2 yellow onions, finely chopped

4 cloves garlic, minced

1-inch piece fresh ginger, peeled and grated or minced

1 small green serrano chile, seeded and minced

2 teaspoons salt

1 (14^1/2-ounce) can crushed tomatoes

1 chicken, cut into serving pieces and skinned

^{1}/4 teaspoon saffron threads

^{1}/2 cup half-and-half

^{1}/4 cup chopped cilantro, for garnish

KEEMA-STUFFED PEPPERS

Serves 4

In Indian cooking, keema *refers to spiced ground meat. Curried potatoes and peas could be substituted for the beef mixture if you prefer a vegetarian version of the dish.*

Combine the cumin, coriander, and cinnamon in a mortar or coffee grinder and grind to a fine powder.

Heat a large sauté pan over medium-high heat and add the oil. Add the onion and sauté, stirring frequently, for 10 minutes, or until lightly browned. Decrease the heat to medium and add the meat. Cook, stirring to break up the meat, for 10 minutes, or until cooked through and lightly browned. Add the garlic and ginger and cook for 3 minutes. Add the spice mixture, turmeric, chile powder, and salt to taste and stir for 2 to 3 minutes. Add the rice and peas and stir well.

Slice the tops off the bell peppers and scoop out the seeds and ribs. Tightly stuff the peppers with the meat mixture and place in the slow cooker.

Cover and cook on low for 4 to 6 hours, until the peppers are soft. Transfer to plates and serve immediately.

TO DRINK Indian beer or a medium-bodied white wine from Spain's Rueda district.

1 teaspoon cumin seed

1 teaspoon coriander seed

1 cinnamon stick, broken into pieces

3 tablespoons vegetable oil

1 large yellow onion, finely chopped

1 pound extra-lean ground beef or lamb

3 large cloves garlic, minced

1-inch piece fresh ginger, peeled and grated or minced

$1/2$ teaspoon ground turmeric

$1/2$ teaspoon pure chile powder

Salt

1 cup cooked rice, quinoa, or potatoes

1 cup fresh or frozen peas

4 large green or red bell peppers

Chicken Stock

Makes 8 cups

Here's a pure chicken stock, made without aromatic vegetables or herbs, for use in a wide variety of slow-cooked dishes. To me, going out and buying a whole chicken for making stock seems a shameless waste of money. I much prefer to stockpile necks, backs, giblets, and other unwanted chicken parts in plastic bags in the freezer until I have enough to make up a batch of stock. An added advantage of making your own stock is that you can refrigerate it overnight and remove most of the congealed fat the next day. In addition, a stock made on the low setting of your slow cooker will be clearer than one that has been brought to a boil on the stove top.

Combine the chicken and water in the slow cooker. Cover and cook on low for about 8 hours, until all the meat has fallen off the bones.

Strain the stock through a medium-meshed sieve into a bowl. Refrigerate overnight, then skim off the congealed fat the next day. Use immediately, refrigerate for up to 3 days, or freeze for up to 3 months.

$2^1/_2$ pounds chicken necks, backs, and giblets

8 cups water

Resources

Most of us rely on our local market for the bulk of our cooking ingredients. But there are always a few producers whose products are superior to those found in most food stores. A few such producers and their products have made a difference in my cooking and enhanced my pleasure in cooking. Here are some of them.

The California Press
Napa Valley, California
(707) 944-0343 • (707) 944-0350 fax
www.californiapress.com
Fine nut oils.

California Press founder John Baritelle had a Piedmontese grandmother, who used to say that "only barbarians use olive oil." Her preference was for the more delicate and refined walnut oil that was pressed every year from their walnut trees in Walnut Creek, California. According to Baritelle, she used her walnut oil like other cooks use butter or olive oil. It was fresh and flavorful, and, as an adult, John longed for the fragrant oils he remembered from his childhood. Unfortunately, the few commercial nut oils he came across were pressed from industrial rejects and were often rancid. What to do but to create his own press and do it right? Baritelle buys walnuts, pecans, hazelnuts, pistachios, and almonds from the best growers in the western United States and cold presses the oils in small batches.

California Press nut oils can be found in specialty stores around the country and can also be mail-ordered directly from the producer. Use them for finishing dishes and salad dressings, or as an ingredient in walnut cake or bread, where their pure, intense flavors can be fully appreciated.

Lundberg Family Farms
5370 Church Street
PO Box 369 • Richvale, CA 95974-0369
(530) 882-4551 • (530) 882-4500 fax
www.lundberg.com
High-quality and organic rices.

The Lundberg family has been producing high-quality, mostly organic rices since 1937, when the patriarch, Albert Lundberg, first decided to farm rice in the Sacramento Valley. The elder Lundberg had seen the ravages of the dust bowl that resulted from poor soil management and short-sighted farming techniques. He and his sons pioneered organic rice growing in the United States.

The Lundbergs grow and sell both organic Arborio rice (traditionally used for risotto) and organic basmati rice (traditional for Indian dishes). In addition, they have some unusual aromatic rices and blends of their own.

MacArthur Beverages
4877 MacArthur Blvd., N.W. • Washington, DC 20007
(202) 338-1433 • www.bassins.com
Greek wines.

MacArthur Beverages has an online catalog and offers a good selection of Greek wines. MacArthur can get you most any Greek wine you want, even if it's not in stock.

Melissa's/World Variety Produce, Inc.

PO Box 21127 • Los Angeles, CA 90021

(800) 588-0151 • www.melissas.com

Specialty produce and dried chiles.

Melissa's is the largest distributor of specialty produce in the United States, with more than eight hundred items to choose from. It also has an excellent selection of high-quality dried chiles and chile powders, and the website gives instructions on handling dried chiles and making your own chile powder. Order from Melissa's either online or by phone.

Penzeys Spices

PO Box 924 • Brookfield, WI 53008-0924

(800) 741-7787 • www.penzeys.com

High-quality spices, herbs, and seasonings.

Penzeys prides itself on offering high-quality spices from around the world at reasonable prices. In addition, mail-ordered spices arrive in good condition and turnover is rapid, so you know you're getting fresh product.

Pop's Wine & Spirits

256 Long Beach Road • Island Park, NY 11558

(516) 431-0025 • www.popswines.com

Greek wines.

Pop's has a wide selection of Greek wines and can obtain any of the wines in this book if not already in stock.

Sea Star Salt

Oakville, California

(888) 767-SALT • www.seastarseasalt.com

Specialty salts.

It isn't the case that salt is just salt. As a product of earth or sea, salt is subject to the same kind of variations in flavor due to location, source, and farming techniques as any other agricultural product.

Sea Star works exclusively with the Brittany salt farmer Sylvain Le Duc, who farms his Celtic gray salt in a traditional centuries-old manner. When the climate is right, he collects the crystals by hand with an ancient tool called a *las*. The salt crystals are formed below the water's surface, not created through evaporation. The salt is then dried by the sun and wind. He ships the fresh salt directly to Sea Star, where it is packaged and sold here in the United States. Sylvain's rigorous practices have earned him France's highest ranking for purity, called "Nature and Progress." You can find Sea Star salt in specialty stores across the country, or you can order direct on the website or by phone.

The Wine Bank

363 Fifth Avenue, Suite 100

San Diego, CA 29101 • (800) 940-9463

Mexican wines.

The Wine Bank is one of the most complete and reliable sources for Mexican wines. It can mail wines to you, provided you live in a state that allows direct shipping of wines.

Zürsun, Ltd., Lola Weyman

Twin Falls, Idaho

(800) 424-8881

Rare and heirloom beans.

Lola Weyman's Cassoulet U.S.A. line of unique and heirloom beans is something that ought not to be missed. Lola is located in Twin Falls, Idaho, and contracts with mostly local growers for forty-three different kinds of beans. At least thirteen varieties are organically grown. Her most popular varieties are cannellini, French green lentils, tiny black lentils, Christmas limas, and flageolets. Her products can be found in many specialty stores or can be mail-ordered directly from Lola.

Index